T0277982

PRAISE FOR *HEART. SOUL. PEN.*

"Robin's unique background in spiritual psychology, women's health, and writing shines through in her teachings. When I began writing, *HEART. SOUL. PEN.* gave me the confidence to believe in myself and my story and write my first book, which changed my life. I would recommend this book to any women who is searching for her voice."
　—Jamie Fiore Higgins, author of *Bully Market: My Story of Money and Misogyny at Goldman Sachs* and named one of the *Financial Times* Top 25 Most Influential Women of 2022

"*HEART. SOUL. PEN.* offers me support and encouragement and a well-defined path to follow with my writing. I always find what I need to keep moving forward. These are tools I go back to over and over again."
　—Melissa Gould, internationally bestselling author of *Widowish*

"Robin Finn's *HEART. SOUL. PEN.* is an absolute gift. The endless guidance and support has helped me push through self-doubt, giving me so much more freedom as a writer. The techniques Robin shares are extremely valuable and have become tools I use every time I sit down to write."
　—Liz Astrof, award-winning executive producer, sitcom writer, and author of *Don't Wait Up: Confessions of a Stay-At-Work Mom*

"In this well-written and easily readable book, *HEART. SOUL. PEN.*, Robin Finn writes about her own story of healing the limiting belief that she wasn't enough. The inherent truth is that we are all enough, regardless of what we may have been taught growing up. Robin takes you, and especially women, on a journey of rediscovering your voice and expressing your creativity through the written word. Her wisdom and beautiful consciousness to be of service to others along with her personal experiences assist others in recognizing their own truth in the worthiness of their being. And what better way to share that than through creative expression. It's a book you'll want to keep close by to read again and again for inspiration."

—Dr. Mary R. Hulnick, codirector and founding faculty of the University of Santa Monica and coauthor of *Loyalty to Your Soul: The Heart of Spiritual Psychology*

"Robin Finn has a gift for instilling confidence and helping you recognize the power of your words. For anyone feeling creatively stuck, the clever writing prompts and thoughtful insights in *HEART. SOUL. PEN.* will remind you that to write is to play."

—Katherine Chang, president of Columbia University Entertainment and writer-producer of Hallmark's *A Brush with Love*

"Midlife is a time of 'ughs and fabulosities.' *HEART. SOUL. PEN.* will help women dig deep to rediscover the power of their authentic voice and unleash the inner sparkle that is uniquely their own. Buckle up, it's time to write and unleash the storyteller within!"

—Dr. Sarah Milken, "The Flexible Neurotic" and host of *The Midlife Reinvention* podcast

"*HEART. SOUL. PEN.* is a book you will return to again and again. I find myself coming back to Robin's wisdom when I feel stuck and need to generate fresh ideas—even when I needed inspiration to write my own wedding vows! The simple steps enable me to focus and connect to the words I want to express from the heart."
—Brooke Jaffe, senior vice president of public affairs and strategy at Penske Media, style expert, trend forecaster, and on-air commentator

"I was in the middle of writing my cookbook *The Vegan ABCs*, when I got stuck on 'M is for Miso.' Using *HEART. SOUL. PEN.*, I let go and wrote from my heart—which led me to create a new format for each letter and I ended up going back to A and starting all over! *HEART. SOUL. PEN.* is a book that will inspire your creativity every time you use it!"
—Lisa Dawn Angerame, author of *Wait, That's Vegan?!* and *The Vegan ABCs Cookbook*

"As a therapist and educator, helping patients and students find their unique voice amid a fast-paced and complicated world is challenging. *HEART. SOUL. PEN.* is that life-affirming book that teaches women the complex process of connecting to their voice in the most approachable and user-friendly way. The results are powerful and life-changing."
—Patty Stegman, LCSW, clinical instructor, NYU Grossman School of Medicine, department of child and adolescent psychiatry

"This book is a gift to women. As a physician specializing in women's healthcare and a working mother, I know firsthand how difficult it is for women to honor themselves by seeking self-care and self-love. For me personally, being a longtime student of *HEART. SOUL. PEN.* has been life-changing both in my personal life and my professional one. I encourage all my patients and my female friends to read this book and follow the simple steps to use writing as a path to self-love and empowerment."

—Rebecca Dupont, MD, obstetrics and gynecology specialist with twenty-eight years of experience

HEART. SOUL. PEN.

HEART.
SOUL.
PEN.

*Find Your Voice on
the Page and in Your Life*

ROBIN FINN

Morehouse Publishing, 19 East 34th Street, New York, NY 10016

Morehouse Publishing is an imprint of Church Publishing Incorporated.

Cover design by Albert Tang
Typeset by Nord Compo

A record of this book is available from the Library of Congress.

ISBN 978-1-64065-707-6 (hardcover)
ISBN 978-1-64065-708-3 (ebook)

For my mother, Vicki Finn,
who lived a life full of color, joy, and style,
and who celebrated the genius inside of everyone she met.
You are my inspiration.

AUTHOR'S NOTE

The names of students who so generously contributed their five-minute writes to this book have been changed to protect their privacy. Thank you so much for sharing your words with me.

CONTENTS

Contents

Contents

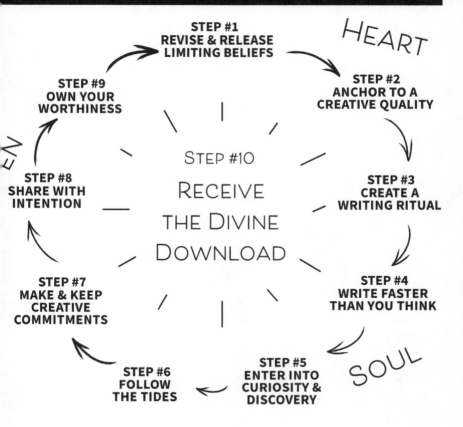

WELCOME TO
HEART. SOUL. PEN.

When I was in the second grade, my teacher arranged all of the kids' desks in small groups, except for mine. My desk was pulled away like a little island in an ocean. Why? Because I was "too social," "too loud," and I "talked too much." I spent the remainder of the year sitting at my desk far away from the rest of the class. At seven years old, I interpreted this to mean: (1) My voice causes humiliation, (2) to be good, I must be quiet, (3) loud girls deserve to be ostracized. I held onto these beliefs for the next thirty-three years.

The messages we receive as kids get lodged inside of us and become lifelong, limiting beliefs that impact how we live, work, write, create, show up in our lives, and relate to ourselves and others. These beliefs limit us from experiencing who we truly are. They keep us small. They keep us from sharing our full expression in the world. Often, we are not aware of these beliefs or certain of their origin.

Many women grow up believing that sharing their voice is not safe or polite or nice. We get the message that if we speak out, we will be punished, ostracized, shamed, humiliated, or make others feel uncomfortable. Then we grow up and become partners, wives, and mothers, in addition to our roles as workers, bosses, sisters, daughters, and friends. Our voices that were already muffled, far away, and hard to hear get buried by all the responsibilities in our lives. Whether or not we are parents or partners, women are trained from birth to put others first and to put ourselves last. We are trained to give and care for others and be selfless. The problem is the longer we put ourselves last, the easier it becomes to lose ourselves altogether. We get so consumed by the needs of others that we no longer connect with our own needs or personal identity.

HEART. SOUL. PEN. is my story of being overwhelmed by parenting, spending two years in an unconventional graduate program in spiritual psychology, and making peace with the voices in my head that told me I was not enough, and it was too late to start writing. Part memoir, part writing manifesto, this is a story about shedding my limiting beliefs, becoming a writer and a teacher, and launching Heart. Soul. Pen.® women's writing workshops to help women reclaim their voices and unleash their radical self-expression. Writing changed my life. It can change yours too.

Have you ever wondered: *How did I end up here? What is my life about? What happened to my dreams? What are my dreams? Who am I apart from everyone else in my life?* It does not matter when this moment strikes: after college or having a baby or leaving a job or leaving a marriage or hitting midlife or facing an empty nest or at retirement. If you have ever woken up and felt like "I have lost my voice," *HEART. SOUL. PEN.* will help you find it again.

Introduction

Too often women want to write but tell me that they are not "real writers," they are not creative, or they do not know what to say. After years of working with women, I can tell you that when women sit down to write and connect to their radical self-expression—the deepest words inside of them—what holds them back is not about writing. It is about worthiness.

It is difficult to express yourself when you believe that your self-expression is uninteresting, silly, unpleasant, or unworthy. Career coach and author Claire Wasserman says in her book *Ladies Get Paid* that for women "to advocate for ourselves out in the world, we have to believe we are worthy of advocacy."[1] With writing, in order to find your voice on the page, you have to believe your voice is worth finding. Otherwise, you end up feeling disheartened and giving up writing altogether.

In this book, I am going to remind you of an inherent truth: what you have to say, share, divulge, and express is important. Writing will transform your life, and now is the time.

It is easy to ignore what we know to be true when we say it to ourselves. It is easy to discount our own advice, doubt our own wisdom, and play small when it is only us watching. I am here to remind you that if you feel the call to write, answer the call. If you want your inner arrow to point toward the direction of your dreams, express yourself. If you feel the words inside pressuring you, let them out.

Writing is a courageous act. I say this all the time and I believe it. I also believe that women who want to write face a twofold challenge: the creative resistance that all writers face and the pervasive judgments about women's value. Women's bodies, beauty, aging, motherhood, midlife, menopause, and everything else related to the female experience are constantly under scrutiny.

For women to unleash our radical self-expression, we have to overcome the resistance that all artists face *and* confront the challenges of the deeply rooted cultural beliefs that live inside of us, keep us small, and have been reinforced our entire lives.

YOU ARE THE EXPERT OF YOUR STORY

In *HEART. SOUL. PEN.,* we are going to examine our beliefs about writing and worthiness. We are going to unpack these beliefs, release them, revise them, and ultimately throw our arms around the fact that we are enough, that what we have to say is enough, that we are worthy of sharing our stories, and that our voices matter.

HEART. SOUL. PEN. is an intuitive process that involves learning strategies and skills to connect to your voice. The premise of this book is that you are the expert of your story. Your wisdom, your words, your knowledge, and your experience will be your guide through these pages. I am here to walk beside you and point out the flowers and the sunset and the edge of the cliff. I will also point out areas where you have already been, and you already know but perhaps have forgotten.

Introduction

You already have a voice, inner wisdom, and an internal GPS. But they may be rusty. I am going to offer specific steps to guide you from a place of uncertainty to a place of greater confidence in your words and in your stories. Along the way, I will remind you that your goal is to stay away from judgment and check in with your intuition. You know what resonates for you. You know which exercises call out, *Do this one!* You know intuitively what your heart needs to hear. Listen to your own wisdom as we progress through the steps. Trust your creative spark.

QUESTIONS ABOUT THE JOURNEY

Here are some questions and answers before we begin our journey:

1. **How does *HEART. SOUL. PEN.* work?** *HEART. SOUL. PEN.* is a step-by-step process designed to help you reclaim your voice, tell your story, and embrace the indisputable value of your life experience and creative self-expression. Women often second-guess their value and believe they are not good enough or that their story is not worthy enough of being shared. This is not true. These are what we call limiting beliefs, designed to keep us safe and silent—we are letting these go.

2. **What is "radical self-expression"?** Radical self-expression is your deepest expression; it is not crafted in your mind but instead bursts forth from the heart and soul. "Radical"

meaning *relating to or affecting the fundamental nature of something; far-reaching or thorough.* When we unleash our radical self-expression, we allow our fundamental nature to pour forth onto the page in words.

3. **Why should I write?** Writing will bring you back to who you are. It will remind you of what is important, what pains you, what your truth is, what your joy is, and everything in between. There are many forms of self-expression which can bring you into connection with yourself. Since I am a writer and this is a book about writing, I am going to walk you through finding your voice on the page. You do not need any writing experience to use this book. All you need is a desire to connect to your voice and a willingness to discover what is percolating inside of you.

4. **What if I am an experienced writer?** If you are an experienced or professional writer looking for a new connection to your creativity, welcome! *HEART. SOUL. PEN.* offers a fresh set of beliefs and inner and outer tools that you may not have used before, or not in a long while.

5. **What if I do not have a "writing project"?** Our writing is never really our project; we are our project and writing is a byproduct. The real project we are working on is ourselves—getting to know and connect to ourselves, while also remembering who we truly are beyond someone else's mother, daughter, spouse, employee, boss, or any other role we play in this world. If you don't have a

writing project, consider "connecting to your voice" as yours.

6. **Should I write with a laptop or pen and paper?** At the beginning of your journey, I recommend forgoing technology-mediated expression (like laptops and tablets), going old school and buying a journal and pen. As your writing becomes easier and more fluid, you may choose to switch to typing on a tablet or computer because it is faster. That is up to you.

7. **What if I am unsure or afraid to write?** If you are worried that your writing is not good enough or that you are not good enough, do not worry. Your writing is good enough. You are good enough. What you have to say has value. The purpose of this book is to stop you from judging your voice. You will hear me say this repeatedly, but judgment is a cork that stops our creative flow and keeps us small and silent. When we judge our writing, we judge it as not good enough. This is not true! It is a limiting belief, which we will talk about more in the pages to come, but the point is, we are leaving the realm of the head and the judgmental mind and entering a space dedicated to curiosity and discovery. We are going to be curious about what we have to say. We are going to discover our radical self-expression. We are going to be willing to believe our words are good enough because they are.

Your *HEART. SOUL. PEN.* journey is broken into three eponymous parts: *HEART, SOUL,* and *PEN*:

- The *HEART* part is where we revise and release our limiting beliefs. In this part, we take a hard look at what we believe to be true about ourselves and our voices and ask if these beliefs support our well-being and creative self-expression. If they don't, we change them or let them go. I spent years working in public health and I can tell you that our beliefs about our well-being directly affect our actions. *Before we write* a single word, we are going to get to the heart of the matter and clean up our belief system and make sure our beliefs support our desire to express ourselves.

- The *SOUL* section is where we allow our words to come forward onto the page without thinking or judging. When I was studying spiritual psychology, my teachers talked about the high-level nature of surrender. To me, surrender sounded like giving up, so I immediately rejected it. But I misunderstood. Surrender is not giving up; *it is giving up control.* In the *SOUL* section, we experience creativity that we didn't know we had and support ourselves *while we write.* In this section, we surrender to our radical self-expression and become curious.

- The *PEN* section is where we consciously decide our next steps *after we write.* We don't allow other people to determine the value of our creativity or what we have to say. We own our value. We do not invite others to comment on our newly lit spark, disrupt our creative process, close our portal, and shut us down. We consciously choose how we want to move through our creative process after we have put pen to paper. In this section, we learn to treat our radical self-expression as a process that is happening in its own perfect time because it is.

YOUR INVITATION

Whether you want to find your voice, deepen your journal writing, write a memoir, publish an essay, launch a blog, pen a novel, write a one-woman show, connect to your personal history, or simply express yourself in writing, *HEART. SOUL. PEN.* is an invitation to show up as yourself on the page.

Every part of you is invited—the pretty parts and the ugly parts, the happy parts and the painful parts, the noisy parts, and the quiet parts. You are invited regardless of your age, stage, marital status, or any other status. You get an A+ in this class just for showing up. Your writing is welcome here, whether it spills out loud and shouted, or tiptoes forward soft and coaxed. Together, we are entering a safe space where we can fully and radically express ourselves. Let's get started . . .

PART I

HEART.

CHANGE YOUR BELIEFS, CHANGE YOUR WRITING

I walked up to the stage wearing black yoga pants, a black sports bra, and a crocheted purple scarf around my waist. The opening notes of *Belly Dance Super Stars, Volume One* filled the room. As a forty-year-old mother of three with a hernia repair and no prior dance experience, I wondered for the millionth time what I was doing. Two hundred classmates sat in purple chairs on the floor in front of me. Two gold hoops hung from my ears. I lifted one hip and then the other and danced onto the stage. I undulated. I shimmied. I rolled my shoulders and attempted some traveling steps. I was not a good belly dancer. But dancing in front of my two hundred classmates was not about being good. It was about being seen.

When I submitted my culminating project for my master's degree program in spiritual psychology, I listed a detailed description of the project and planned completion date. My project focused on traveling and exploring, reading books about adventures, and learning to belly dance. My advisor provided supportive feedback on my proposal. She added in a purple bubble at the bottom of the page:

Robin, please plan on a three-minute dance performance during the final weekend.

Wait, what? I did not know the project included a live dance performance! Dancing was not something I wanted to do in front of my entire class. I felt like "learning to belly dance" had chosen me, not the other way around. I was not a good dancer. I hated performing.

I was a head person, not a heart person. I looked inside my head for answers. I looked inside my head for inspiration and to try to "figure out" who I was and why I was on the planet and what my life was about—besides parenting kids with ADHD and fighting with my children's schools. After years of searching, I reached no conclusions. I started to despair. I didn't know who I was or what I wanted to say. I felt trapped in my head. But I did not know there was anywhere else to be.

Then I started studying spiritual psychology. Then I learned to belly dance. Then I began to write after decades of not writing. The final performance (in front of two hundred classmates and in a purple hip scarf, no less) was not a lesson in belly dancing; it was a lesson in exposure. I just didn't know it yet.

That final performance required I stand on stage and be seen. I had to show up as myself. I had to be vulnerable. I wanted people to see me, but I was terrified at the same time. What if no one liked me? What if I didn't like me? What if I was rejected? What if I messed up? What if I made a fool of myself? What if people laughed? The list of fears went on and on. I felt like I was *not enough*—not good enough, not talented enough, not coordinated enough, not worthy enough of walking out in front of my entire class and belly dancing. Whether on the stage or on the page, the feeling of unworthiness is paralyzing.

I encounter this phenomenon time and again in the *Heart. Soul. Pen.* women's writing workshops I teach. Women tell me they are *not enough* in so many ways: their stories are not important enough, they are not good enough writers or *real* writers, or no one will care about what they have to say. These limiting beliefs keep women silent, keep their voices from being heard, and keep them from connecting to the radical self-expression that is inside and wants to be liberated.

THE MYTH OF THE MUNDANE

At a recent writing workshop, a women raised her hand to share her writing. When I called on her, she told the group that she did not want to read her piece out loud because she said, "It's so mundane." With gentle encouragement, she shared a piece about caregiving for her husband who was newly diagnosed with Parkinson's disease. She wrote about how she sometimes did not feel like caregiving, and how difficult it was to care for him and herself, and how hard and painful it was to adjust to a new life with his illness. Not only was the writing not mundane, but it was brave, important, poignant, and relatable to anyone who has ever cared for a loved one with an illness. Her piece was filled with grief, truth, loss, and hope.

As a teacher, I find this happens all the time—women tell me they have nothing "important" to say and then, when encouraged, share writing full of so much longing, loss, joy, pain, and yearning that it takes my breath away. When I ask the class, "Was this uninteresting?" they laugh. It seems funny to ask the question because it is so obvious that the writing has illuminated some important aspect of being human and that the writer has boldly shared it with us. The bottom line is that we are moved by each other's authentic self-expression. In our highly curated social media world, people are hungry for truth. But we cannot get to the truth when we judge it as not enough.

I could say that I do not know where women get the message that they are not enough or that their writing does not have value. But that would be a lie. As a woman, of course I do. Women get the message that they are not enough or that their words or self-expression are not important from just about everywhere. We are told to be pleasant. To not be bossy, loud, or make other people feel uncomfortable. We are told to be sunny, to smile, to be positive and reassuring. We are told not to talk about the excruciating nature of motherhood, midlife, menopause, mental health, sexual violence, sexual desire, or anything that is not "pretty." And, when we become a mother or get older or hit midlife or go gray (or silver), then we really should be quiet since "we are not in our prime" (as if someone else gets to determine when we are in our prime). Add to this the misbeliefs placed on young girls that they should not be demanding, or too talkative, or take up too much space, or else they are not "good." Just like me in second grade, these beliefs can stick to us for years, decades even.

Is it any wonder that so many women think they do not have anything of value to say, or that they are not worthy enough to say it?

ALIGNMENT

Too often, we want to find our voice and we do not want to find our voice *at the same time.* Fear of exposure is a powerful barrier. We have to be willing to give up the beliefs that keep us small, that do not serve us, that tell us we are not enough, if we want to unleash our words and our radical self-expression with ease. It is difficult to believe that we have nothing worthwhile to say and still write.

The trick is to align our beliefs with our goals. If our goal is to write and connect with our words, we can create beliefs about writing that support us. If we yearn to find our voice, we can remove the barriers that keep our voice from emerging. If our dream is to develop a vibrant writing practice and share our work with the world, we can construct a belief system that supports living our dream.

You are enough. What you have to say is enough. What you want to share is enough. Whatever education level or life experience or background you have, that is enough. You are worthy of writing your story. Because you are. This is The Truth. Any voice that tells you otherwise—that you're not worthy or not good enough or not anything enough—is a limiting belief.

Truth Resonates

I trained as a public health worker, and I saw firsthand how beliefs affect behavior. One of my first jobs in public health was at the New York City Department of Health Bureau of Tuberculosis (TB) Control. I created educational videos to help patients with TB understand that they could recover from TB with medication. Patients who did not believe they could get better were much less likely to stay on a long, complicated treatment regimen than those who thought they would recover with treatment.

What we believe affects how we behave. Writing is no different. We are much more likely to keep writing when we trust that we are creative, our words are worthwhile, and we have something of value to share.

What do we believe about ourselves? This can be a tough question because we may not know, or we may be afraid to look. As I talked about earlier, beliefs can originate in childhood and lurk inside our heads for decades without us even being aware. In the *HEART* section, we bring our beliefs to light. What we believe is more important than how much natural talent we have or how experienced we are as writers or how many writing classes we have or have not taken. What we believe about ourselves is critical to what we can achieve.

The *HEART* section takes place before we write because we are setting ourselves up for success. In this section, we are going to challenge our beliefs and change our relationship to ourselves. When we change our relationship to ourselves, our relationship to writing can't help but evolve.

CHAPTER ONE

STEP #1–REVISE AND RELEASE LIMITING BELIEFS

I remember my father. I wear his wedding ring on my pointer finger. I remember the sound of his voice and the jeans he used to wear and the white sneakers on his feet as he stepped into the canal to push the boat off the trailer and into the water so we could go fishing. I remember once how I came home late, like two in the morning, and I saw my father's car was not on the driveway. I knew he was driving around looking for me. I knew I was in big trouble. I was glad he did not find me behind Wags smoking weed with a police officer I met at a party he had come to break up. We got to talking, and the next thing I know, we were behind Wags smoking a joint. I do not know what would have made my dad angrier, the hour or the pot or the police officer. Actually, I do know: the police officer. I am glad I did not get caught behind Wags with Officer What's-his-name. I don't remember.

—Rachel H.
Prompt: *I remember*
Timer: 5 minutes

MY WRITING JOURNEY

When I was a kid, I was a journal writer and budding poet. I submitted a poem to the Broward County Youth Fair and won a red ribbon. Later I wrote short sci-fi stories, and my eighth-grade teacher sent them to our state representative who congratulated me on my future as a writer. I wrote for fun and creative self-expression and, back then, it did not occur to me to question whether my writing was good or not.

In college, I planned on majoring in English but because of graduation requirements, I ended up a political science major. After college, I went into public health and left writing behind. As I look at my career, I was always drawn to the aspects of writing in any job I had. But I gave up the thought of being a *writer* because it seemed impractical, and I didn't have the confidence that I could do it. I noticed that as I got older, whenever I sat down to write in a journal, I struggled to write. I had no flow.

Somehow writing had become hard and not fun. I did not know what I wanted to say. I had lost the thread to the ideas that used to spark and unroll right from my pen easily onto the page. I got a job, worked, got married, had a baby, and forgot all about writing. But sometimes I would feel the urge to write. I would want to express myself, but I would quash the feeling and do something else. I did not find writing fun because it seemed too hard, frustrating, and unsatisfying.

MOTHERHOOD

Fast-forward to motherhood: I had three kids and an expectation of how my life should be. My children would be easy, I would be a great mother, my house would be clean, and we'd have a yard with a white picket fence. But that's not how it turned out—except for the white picket fence. It turned out that one of my kids had severe ADHD and the other two were out-of-the-box learners. Parenting was not easy and having a kid with severe ADHD required full-time advocacy. I spent so much time fighting for accommodations, fighting with the school, and fighting for my kids that all that fighting wore me out.

During those years my main feeling about myself was FAILURE. I dreamed of a vibrant career but as a mother of three, including a child with special needs, even taking on freelance work was difficult. I dreamed of a peaceful environment where the kids followed my directions but corralling them was hard. I thought I would be good at everything, but I didn't feel good at anything. I was lost. I had no anchor to myself.

I thought about the last time I felt good and all I could think about was school. I decided to investigate psychology and consider going back to school to earn a master's degree. As I was researching programs that offered night or weekend classes, I met three different people who all earned master's degrees in spiritual psychology from the same school, the University of Santa Monica (USM). I had no idea what spiritual psychology was. But I realized the strangeness of three random people coming into my life and mentioning the same program, so I went to an information session.

The graduates discussed the transformative nature of studying spiritual psychology. They talked about reconnecting to themselves and discovering aspects of who they were that they never knew before. I was hooked. Before I left that evening, I registered for the two-year program to earn a master's degree.

What is spiritual psychology? It is an area of psychology that focuses on personal growth and teaches tools to release thoughts and patterns that no longer serve in order to create the life we desire. As I mentioned before, I had dreams about what my life was going to look like, but nothing turned out like I planned. I judged myself as having failed at the most important job I would ever have: being a mom. I believed that a good mom could fix her family. Since I couldn't heal mine, I was not a good mom. I was a failure. With these beliefs, is it any wonder I was filled with shame and anxiety? My mental and physical well-being suffered. I felt drained.

Through spiritual psychology, I came to understand the concept of "limiting beliefs." Limiting beliefs (also called *misbeliefs*) are judgments or misinterpretations of reality that hold us back or limit what we can do, be, or achieve. They were ruining my life without me being aware and making it impossible for me to feel good about myself, enjoy parenting, or connect to other people. My misbeliefs made me feel like I needed to fight to be heard. They also made me hide because I was afraid other people would see what a failure I was.

LIMITING BELIEFS 101

One of the most powerful breakthroughs I had while studying spiritual psychology was that I could change my belief system.[1]

I learned that I could consciously identify, revise, and release any beliefs I had that did not serve me, made me miserable, or held me back. I did not have to hold onto beliefs from second grade. I did not need to cling to beliefs created at PTA meetings that I needed to do more than I was already doing. I did not need to hold onto beliefs that other parents placed on me about how kids with ADHD should behave. These realizations changed everything.

I discovered that my beliefs dictated my life. When I changed my beliefs, my life experience changed. That is how powerful and predictive inner beliefs are: they dictate your inner thoughts as well as your outer experience.

At the time, my main role was *mother,* and, as mentioned earlier, I believed I was failing at that responsibility. Armed with a new emotional toolkit from my studies, I decided to identify, revise, and release my limiting beliefs around motherhood. Almost overnight, I felt like a more conscientious and present mother. Suddenly, the possibility of achieving a feeling of joy in my family life seemed realistic.

This was my step-by-step process:

1. I wrote down my beliefs about parenting and motherhood and success. Here were mine when I got started:
   - A good mother fixes her family.
   - If I cannot fix my family or force them to be different, I am a bad mother.

- Parenting success is measured by my kids' ability to fit in.

- If I fail as a mother, I have no worth or value.

- I better not let anyone see me or they will know I suck as a mom and a person.

2. I reviewed each belief according to two main questions:

   - Does this belief support my goal to enjoy motherhood and my life?

   - Does this belief make me feel good—is it uplifting?

3. If the answer to both questions was "yes," I kept the belief. If the answer to either question in whole or in part was "no," I revised it or released it.

4. I created new beliefs that supported my goal to feel good in my life and to view myself as a conscientious mother. Here were my beliefs when I finished:

   - I am doing the best I can.

   - It is not my job to fix anybody.

   - Nobody is broken.

   - A good mother loves and accepts herself and her family while they struggle.

   - There is no such thing as parenting success or failure, there is simply loving and accepting your family and yourself as you struggle.

   - I am a divine being having a parenting experience.

- I have a learning orientation toward life.
- I have compassion for myself.

5. For months, I repeated my new beliefs daily, made them the screen saver on my iPhone, read them before bed, and when I woke up.

While creating a new belief system gave me a sense of relief right away, I did not immediately embrace these new beliefs. It took time. That is why it is called a "practice." I had to practice daily. I would catch myself falling into my old limiting beliefs and I would need to read, review, and accept my new beliefs over and over again. The more I repeated the new beliefs, the more comfortable I became with them. Eventually, they simply became my new belief system.

I was elated. No more fighting! No more struggling! Okay, I am exaggerating: after I adopted my new belief system about parenting, my life was not perfect, but it improved immensely. I went from feeling small, frustrated, and alone to full of possibility, peace, and acceptance. Although nothing in the outer world changed, I changed. My children still had learning differences and I was still an outlier and an advocate, but I accepted and supported myself. And, slowly, the outer world shifted too. Allies and friends materialized where they had not been before.

Parenting taught me the power of revising and releasing beliefs that no longer served me. I thought this lesson would change my life and it did. But learning is a process, not an event. I did not *get it* and then acquire Buddha-like wisdom about everything in my life. I *got it* and then had to keep getting it over and over again as I faced new and different challenges. Which brings me to writing . . .

LIMITING BELIEFS ABOUT WRITING AND WORTHINESS

After I completed my spiritual psychology program, I wanted to take a writing class. Writing had been calling me for years, but I resisted. Every time I thought about it, I always came up with reasons why the timing was not right. After I earned my master's degree, I decided now was the time. I was forty years old. The last thing I wrote for myself was a letter that was published in *The Daily Bruin* during my senior year at UCLA. So I did it. I enrolled in a ten-week writing class, grabbed a notebook, and headed downtown.

When I arrived, I sat in a circle with the other students while the teacher gave us a prompt. I thought about it for a while and eventually wrote something. Then we went around the circle and shared. I felt embarrassed, uncomfortable, mortified. One guy penned a comedy sketch. Another person had beautiful prose. I mumbled through my turn, loathing the words I had written about how I hated cooking and the fight I had with my kid's teacher. The feedback made my face itch and my hands sweat. Not because it was negative, but simply because it underscored my feelings of insecurity and worthlessness. When I got to the car, I dropped my bag on the seat and felt the tears well up. I quit the class.

I did not want to write about parenting, motherhood, or the gnawing ambition inside my stomach that would never be satisfied. But this is what wanted to be written. It demanded to be written, even if, to me, the topics felt worthless. How did the class go so wrong? Why did I leave in such despair?

The issue was not writing; it was shame. Shame is a powerful barrier to self-expression. I wanted to write and express myself, but there was so much judgment holding me back. I felt ashamed of how little value there was in my writing. The pressure between my desire to express myself and the judgment holding it in made me miserable.

But this time I could feel the limiting beliefs inside of me. I knew they were there. I knew that I held judgments against myself. I knew that I did not believe I was a *real* writer. I knew that I thought everyone else was cooler and smarter and way more interesting than me, a middle-aged mother of three. I knew it and I could feel it and I knew I had to face it.

I had wanted to write my entire life. I was born a writer. I had been trying to express myself for years. It was now or never. I could not keep using my kids, my lack of experience, my carpool duties, my grocery list, or my laundry folding as an excuse not to write. If I wanted to start, I had to do it now. I had a decision to make. So, I sat down and investigated my beliefs again. This time, I focused on my beliefs about writing and worthiness.

This was my step-by-step process:

1. I examined my beliefs about writing and worthiness by writing down each belief. Mine looked like this:

   - Only young, hip people have something to say.
   - I am too old to write.

- It is too late.
- My writing is embarrassing.
- The topics I am writing about are boring.
- No one will care about what I am writing.
- I am not a good writer.
- I should stop trying.
- If I keep writing, everyone will see I am not good enough.
- I missed my chance.

2. I reviewed each belief according to two main questions:
   - Does this belief support my goal to write, express myself, unleash my radical self-expression?
   - Does this belief make me feel good—is it uplifting?

3. If the answer to both questions was "yes," I kept the belief. If the answer to either question in whole or in part was "no," I revised or released it.

4. I created new beliefs that supported my goal to write and express myself. Here were my beliefs when I finished:
   - I write because I feel called.
   - I am naturally creative.
   - Writing is an adventure.
   - I am curious about what words will emerge.
   - I give myself permission to write what is true for me.

- I am worthy of hearing and expressing myself.
- I am safe.
- I am allowed to be seen.
- It is enough to show up and write.
- I am enough.
- Now is the perfect time.
- I have compassion for myself.

5. For months, I repeated my new beliefs daily, made them the screen saver on my phone, reread them before I went to bed and when I woke up.

Getting rid of my limiting beliefs about writing, about myself as a writer, and about my own worthiness gave me the sense of relief I experienced when I used the same approach to parenting. But, like before, it also took time to fully embrace these new beliefs. Still, I felt calmer, more inspired, and even excited. I felt ready to begin a fresh writing adventure.

Have you ever heard the saying: *When the student is ready, the teacher appears?* I decided to look for a new writing class and found one in my neighborhood with a teacher who had studied spiritual psychology! Voila! It felt like I ordered the class off a Divine menu. This time, I showed up with my new beliefs intact. I let go of thinking that my writing had to be hip or cool or anything but simply mine. Writing became a kind of compass I could use to explore the parts of myself I had never encountered or did not know about. My new teacher's gentle encouragement and nonjudgmental presence helped me come alive on the page.

Seven years later, I was a widely published essayist. One of the first articles I pitched was to the parenting editor of Buzz-Feed. It was a list-article called "28 Things Nobody Tells You about Having a Kid with ADHD." When I pitched him, I felt nauseous. When it was published, I thought I might throw up. When it went viral, I was terrified. But this time, I recognized the terror for what it was: the fear of being seen. The essay was about parenting a kid with severe ADHD, which was what my life was about. The voice in my head said, "How dare you show yourself." I remembered the belly dancing. I stood in front of my bathroom mirror and told myself, "You can do this." And I did. My inbox blew up with emails from readers sharing their experiences parenting kids with ADHD and thanking me for making them feel less alone.

If I had listened to my limiting beliefs, parents around the world would continue to suffer alone. But they were not alone. I was having this experience too. I knew the pain, frustration, and hope of raising a child with ADHD. Writing at its best helps us connect to each other and feel less isolated in our individual lives.

HOW LIMITING BELIEFS AFFECT WRITERS

Limiting beliefs limit our capabilities. If we want to find our voice, write with abandon, or allow our thoughts and ideas to flow onto the page, we have to stop and look at the beliefs we hold about writing *before* we start writing. If we do not take the time to identify, revise, and release limiting beliefs, writing often goes like this:

1. You feel the creative spark or a strong call to write. Some story or seed or idea wants to come out and be expressed. You are excited to write.

2. You buy a new journal, enroll in a writing class, or commit to set aside time to work on a bubbling story, poem, or essay, or simply let out your thoughts on the page. You feel inspired. You begin to write.

3. You read what you wrote and judge it. You decide it is not good. Or you like it and share it with a friend, teacher, or writing group and the feedback you get confuses you or undermines your belief in the idea. You had the best of intentions but now you struggle and freeze.

4. You stop writing.

5. You give up.

When I talk with students who have encountered this phenomenon, they tell me that, deep down, they did not feel their story was *enough*—not big enough or important enough or worthy enough—to justify spending time writing about it. They tell me they felt they did not have the authority, wisdom, talent, or commitment to write it. They tell me that giving up made them miserable because they deeply wanted to write, but they could not muster the energy or focus or inspiration to keep going. I tell them that writing while holding limiting beliefs about writing is hard. But that does *not* mean you should give up your writing. It means you should give up your limiting beliefs.

When women show up at my writing workshops, they commonly tell me:

- "I've lost my voice."
- "I feel like I'm hiding out from myself."
- "I feel like I don't want to be seen."
- "I feel like, in some ways, I have given up."
- "My life force is dulled."
- "I can't express myself."
- "I want to write for myself, but I don't know where to start."
- "I feel like I'm just toiling away at nothing."
- "I don't know what to write about."
- "I haven't written in years."
- "I'm not a real writer."
- "I am too old, too late, too tired to start."
- "No one will care about this."
- "Writing terrifies me."
- "I can't write anything personal."
- "I am not creative."
- "I used to be creative."
- "I used to have direct access to my creativity but not anymore."

- "I haven't written since I was sixteen."
- "It's just journaling."

In addition, society sends gendered messages to women about the value of their stories. These messages suggest women's stories are not important, women's issues are taboo/inappropriate/should remain hidden, women's experiences are not interesting, particularly those of older women. These messages look like:

- Whoops, woman over thirty, you're past your prime.

- Midlife women, you are too old to start writing or to keep writing or to write anything anyone wants to read.

- You are a mother? People are not interested in your child-rearing stories or how hard it is to parent or how tired you are of making the same meal every day for three years for picky eaters or that you won't eat cake at your birthday party because you're afraid of gaining weight or how crazy your own mother made you feel.

- No one wants to hear about period pain or pregnancy or menopause. Please keep your bodily functions and your hot flashes, night sweats, and meno-fog to yourself.

- Abortion, sexual assault, and workplace discrimination are hot button issues: you better proceed carefully.

- Your story is boring and/or we have heard it before, so we don't need to hear it again.

Here is what I know about limiting beliefs. We all have them. There are different versions and often originate in childhood or when we are young, but essentially, all say the same thing: you are not good enough so stop writing. They keep us small and quiet. They force us to give up. They plague women by playing on our fears that we are "not enough." They shut us down. They are designed to protect us and keep us safe from harm. They are not true.

Ten Truths You Need to Know about Yourself as a Writer

1. You are enough.
2. What you have to say is enough.
3. Whatever you have to give is enough.
4. Whatever time you have is enough.
5. Your voice is unique.
6. Your story matters.
7. You are the only one who can tell your story.
8. Now is the perfect time.
9. You have everything you need.
10. Writers write. If you are writing, you are a writer.

FEAR OR FLOW: CHOOSE ONE

If judgment is a cork that holds our stories inside, then fear is a waist-high field of mud that drags us down. When we believe we are not enough—not smart enough, good enough, talented enough, young enough, important enough, or whatever enough—writing feels like walking through deep mud. Every leg lift is tiring, every step is arduous, every inch feels like a mile. You *can* get through the mud, but it requires a Herculean effort, and it takes forever.

We can write with fear, but it is slow and full of effort. We are writing against our own impulse to protect ourselves. Each sentence can be a challenge to get out. If we want our words to *flow*, we have to be willing to give up our limiting beliefs. We can have flow or fear but not both.

THE VOW NEVER TO DISPARAGE

In workshops, students often want to preface their writing before they share it, but I do my best to stop them. Why? Because I know—I know!—they are not going to preface their work by saying, "I am so proud of this piece," or "This is amazing," or "This piece of writing felt like a revelation." I am certain what they are going to say is, "This does not make sense," or "I was really tired this morning," or "I don't know what I wrote," or "It is not good."

One of the key tenets of *HEART. SOUL. PEN.* is to never disparage your creative process, including your writing, your stories, and how much creative work you are able to get done on a regular basis. For some people, this will feel very uncomfortable. It is amazing how difficult it can be to give up the practice of cutting ourselves down. It's as if our default is to criticize ourselves and tear down our work. Simply put, this is not helpful to our creative process. Disparaging our work does not encourage us to trust our creative spark. It makes us second-guess ourselves, doubt our value, belittle our expertise, and sabotage the joy that radical self-expression brings. Harsh critique shuts us down.

It is far more effective to your writing process to approach yourself with gentleness, monitor how you speak to yourself, and lean into the new, supportive beliefs you created. I tell my students: either be neutral or do not say anything but do not be negative. (The other option is to simply embrace the magnificence of your own unique creative voice.)

We can move away from the impulse to disparage ourselves, our writing, or our writing process and move into a more supportive and gentle relationship with ourselves by consciously committing to change. We do this by creating a *Vow Never to Disparage*, signing it, and pasting the *Vow* somewhere where it will always be visible when we sit down to write. We formalize the *Vow* and sign it so that we make a commitment to not disparage our creative process. This may take vigilance, but we can do it with some effort and attention.

Taking the time to prepare your belief system *before you write* pays off. Revising and releasing limiting beliefs helps open the creative portal through which our deepest creative self-expression travels. Taking a *Vow Never to Disparage* keeps that portal open. When the creative portal is squeezed tightly, it is hard to get the words out. You can do it, but it is that writing-through-mud feeling again. Nothing squeezes the creative portal closed more than judgment. Commit to letting go of disparaging yourself as part of your creative process. If you cannot think or say something positive about yourself or your work, then simply remain neutral about what is emerging.

AFTER THE DANCE

When I look back on my belly dance performance, I remember wrapping the lavender scarf around my waist. I heard the opening notes of *Belly Dance Super Stars, Volume One*, and, a few minutes later, walked off the stage amazed at what I had accomplished. I can't recall how well I danced or if I got all the steps right. But I'll never forget the email I received from a classmate a few days later. She wrote:

> *Your belly dance performance gave me the courage to improvise and dance freely in the middle of a circle of friends at a party last night. It felt incredibly liberating to allow myself to dance in front of others the way I dance alone in my house. It is true that "Playing small does no good for you or others. When you allow yourself to shine, you give others permission to do the same." This is what your performance did for me. Thank you so very much.*

Our writing has the same effect. When we express our authentic truth, we give others permission to do the same.

CHAPTER TAKEAWAYS

- Spiritual psychology teaches tools to release thoughts and patterns that no longer serve in order to create the life we desire.

- Limiting beliefs (also called *misbeliefs*) are judgments and misinterpretations of reality that hold us back or limit what we can do, be, or achieve.

- Limiting beliefs can run our lives even if we do not know it.

- Our beliefs dictate our inner thoughts as well as our outer experiences.

- Disparaging ourselves makes us second-guess our writing, doubt our value, belittle our expertise, and sabotage the joy that radical self-expression brings.

- When we express our authentic truth, we give others permission to do the same.

EXERCISE: HOW TO REVISE AND RELEASE LIMITING BELIEFS

Let's go through the process of reviewing your beliefs about writing, identifying the beliefs that don't serve your goals, and revising or releasing them so that the beliefs you actively hold support the goals you want to achieve. In other words, let's change your beliefs. Follow these simple steps to get started:

1. Write down your beliefs about writing and self-expression and worthiness.

2. Review each belief according to two questions:

   • Does this belief support my goal to write, express myself, unleash my radical self-expression?

   • Does this belief make me feel good—is it uplifting?

3. If the answer to both questions is "yes," keep the belief. If the answer to either question in whole or in part is "no," revise it or release it.

4. Create new beliefs that support your writing, your worthiness, and your radical self-expression.

5. Write them down and review them. Do they support your goals? If not, go back to #4. If so, go on to #6.

6. Repeat your new beliefs daily. Read them once in the morning and once at night at a minimum.

Reminder: We may not initially believe our new, more supportive beliefs. That is okay. The more we repeat the new beliefs and anchor to them, the more comfortable we will feel. It takes time. That is why it is called a "practice." We have to practice every day until our new beliefs become ingrained within us as part of our identity.

EXERCISE: TAKE THE VOW NEVER TO DISPARAGE

Create a vow in which you commit to refrain from disparaging yourself or your creative process. Promise to be kind to yourself, refrain from apologizing for your self-expression, and give up making excuses. Acknowledge that your fresh, newly written material contains the seeds of future stories. Promise that when reviewing your words, you will avoid judging them or saying bad things about yourself or your work. Remind yourself that trusting your creative spark means letting go of the need to judge. Write down your *Vow Never to Disparage*, sign it, and keep it. Below is a sample:

VOW NEVER TO DISPARAGE

I commit to never disparaging my work. I will not say anything mean, negative, or dismissive about my writing, my writing process, or my creativity. I will not make faces nor use harsh words. I will not sigh loudly. I will not talk about "shitty" first drafts or bad writing or how hard writing is. I will say neutral or positive things about my writing and my creative process. Otherwise, I will remain silent. I am making this vow and keeping it.

Signature:

Date:

CHAPTER TWO

STEP #2–ANCHOR TO A CREATIVE QUALITY

I remember when flying used to be a pleasure. The only thing we had to contend with was inclement weather. I remember methodically planning trips with excitement and anticipation. Now, I do a balance transfer, borrow points, and redeem my vacation. I remember looking through my closet to choose a fabulous airplane outfit. These days, I don comfy jeggings, Uggs, and blanket to stave off being frostbit. I remember flying Eastern Airlines, checking bags, and eating a full meal, all for one-inclusive fare. Today, I had to pay for my seat, carry-on, legroom, and a box full of nuts. I remember chatting with my flight mates, collecting business cards, or happily looking out the window. Here, no connection, technology over humanity, plugged-in seatmate hitting me with his elbow. I remember wearing belts and shoes, paper tickets, meeting or greeting loved ones at the gate. This morning, at JFK, even with TSA pre-check, I was scanned twice and there were armed soldiers poised to keep us safe. I remember traveling with ease, hope, tomato juice, and without panic disorder.

—Isabel E.
Prompt: *I remember*
Timer: 5 minutes

How My Quality Entered My Life

When I began my program in spiritual psychology, our teacher took us on a guided meditation. I sat in my chair, closed my eyes, and listened to her voice:

> *I was on the beach, walking in the surf. I looked out at the ocean and could see curly whisps of white foam as they struggled toward the shore. And then, as I walked, I came to a treasure chest. I dropped to my knees to investigate. The chest was closed so I unlatched it and lifted the heavy lid. Inside was a single starfish sitting on a sheet of red velvet. I lifted the starfish and turned it over. In its small mouth I saw a crumpled piece of paper. I pried it out and unraveled the paper. In my mind, I saw one word written in bold printed letters: HUMOR.*

The closed-eye process was over. Everyone had received their Quality.

People were aglow. I looked around the room and asked others what Quality they had received. People said things like Impeccability, Expansiveness, or Equanimity. I thought maybe I got the wrong one. I wanted something extraordinary, but all I got was Humor. I went to talk to my teacher.

"I think I got the wrong Quality," I told her. "What did you receive?" she asked. "Humor," I said. She laughed and said, "Oh Robin, Humor is majestic. You can't receive the wrong

Quality. Humor is a way to connect to life and to others. I think it's perfect."

As happened with so much that I learned while studying spiritual psychology, I did not get the lesson at the time. It was only later that I understood the gift that Humor bestowed upon me. In fact, humor changed my life when I embraced it.

What is a Quality? Qualities are aspects of our spirit that are always available to support, nurture, and uplift us. The problem is that we forget we can summon them as needed, at any time.

With *HEART. SOUL. PEN.,* before writing, we have the opportunity to choose a Quality to support us for that writing session, moment, workshop, week, month, or eternally. Humor is, was, and always will be one of my Qualities. I hold it close because I recognize that even though it wasn't what I expected, it was meant for me.

You do not need someone else to bestow your Quality upon you. You can give yourself the support you need for your creative self-expression. Too often we write and while we are writing, we are determining that our words are not good, that our story is stupid, that our self-expression has no value. Once we revise our limiting beliefs and replace them with new, supportive beliefs, we are on our way. Then we take the *Vow Never to Disparage* and let go of badmouthing our creative process.

Now, we are ready to anchor to a creative Quality that we can wrap around ourselves like a blanket to keep us from falling into traps of self-doubt and unworthiness.

Summoning the Support You Need

When you pick your Quality, consider what you need. Is it Courage? Or Belief in Self? Is it Focus or Energy or Flow or Perspective or See the Beauty? Every time we sit down to choose a Quality, we are presented again with the opportunity to anchor to an aspect of our spirit that works for us, uplifts us, and reminds us of the importance of what we have to share.

It is not the Quality itself that is life-changing. What is life-changing is remembering that we can choose how we frame our creative struggle. When I began writing again, I was overwhelmed with parenting and life. I felt like I had to multitask every minute of every day and there was so much to do and very little time to get anything done. Sometimes I wanted to scream. Humor helped me laugh instead of cry. It saved me.

Later, as my kids got older, I had more time. I thought I could devote that time to writing. I fantasized about luxurious hours of creativity, but in all that peace and quiet, I could not focus. I had no idea how to live without juggling ten activities at once. This is where choosing a new Quality came in.

I thought of my Quality like a life raft I could hoist myself into that would keep me buoyant, give me structure, and provide support. Your Quality is your life raft. If you let it, it will support you. Your Quality can be different at different times of your life, or it may stay the same for weeks, months, or years. Instead of sitting at home with all this time and no idea what to do with it, I decided to choose a new Quality.

I was coming off years of parenting three kids and needing to get things done. Humor helped me laugh at myself and the crazy situations I had to navigate on a regular basis. In writing, Humor was the anchor that allowed me to dive deep into painful places. But times had changed. Now I sat down to write in a quieter house than I was used to. There were fewer kid duties. My children were growing up and I needed to recalibrate. When I thought about what I needed *now* to support my creative process, I understood that I wanted to shed the need to *get things done* and cultivate the joy of doing. I wanted to engage with enthusiasm and only pursue actions that I felt enthusiastic about. I chose Enthusiasm as my new Quality to remind me to engage in ways that brought me less drudgery and more joy.

Qualities function in different ways. They are part of an intuitive process that helps you determine what *you* need. Sometimes when you are writing, you may encounter material in your work that you do not want to write about. It may be a loss you are still grieving, a conflict that is unresolved, a painful trauma from your past. When difficult material bubbles up, there is an opportunity to choose a Quality to support you creatively. Sometimes, it is Gentleness to allow yourself the space to tackle the material later when you are ready. If you feel ready to write through it but need support, you can choose Strength or Brave Heart or Warrior or Courage. You can write your Quality on a sticky note, paste it on your laptop, or write it on an index card and decorate it with colored markers to remind you that you can do this.

The point of your Quality is to anchor to what you need in the moment to connect to your creative process. Maybe it's Focus because you are distracted. Maybe it's Energy because you feel tired. Maybe it's Acceptance or Peace or Strength. It is up to you.

Once in a workshop, as we were choosing Qualities to prepare to write, a participant said, "Does my writing need to get done?" We dug deeper to better understand what her question was all about. The student was a mother of two, including a child with autism who required an extraordinary level of advocacy. Her writing was painful, powerful, and full of wisdom. She was tired. Her time for herself was limited. Her question generated deep discussion amongst the group.

I asked her whether her writing kept her sane or was another to-do. Did she need a break or had she wandered into a minefield in her writing and was afraid to take another step? There was no right or wrong answer. She thought about these questions and said, "My writing needs to get done, but I need a Quality to support me right now." We brainstormed together about what felt intuitively uplifting to her in this moment. She named what she needed: Acceptance.

Choosing a Quality is about summoning support. It's about marshalling your forces. It's about going through a sifting process to name what you need and then anchoring to it. There is no right or wrong Quality. There is simply what speaks to you in the moment to support your creative process, to give you the strength you need to write what wants to be written, and to connect you to your voice when it is easy and when it is hard.

Step #2—Anchor to a Creative Quality

THE DECK OF QUALITIES

As writers, knowing *what we need* can feel elusive, nameless, and hard to pin down. It is not easy to recognize when we are dealing with our own limiting beliefs or doubt or fear or judgment. It can be harder to recognize the support we need to overcome these obstacles. The Deck of Qualities helps you understand and identify the Quality you need to support your creative process.

We have the support we crave inside of us, but too often it's obscured by exhaustion, shame, and other distractions of everyday life. When we summon a Quality to support our creative work, we anchor ourselves to our authentic voice. We simply need to identify and communicate our Quality out loud.

In *Heart. Soul. Pen.* writing workshops, each student chooses a Quality to open the writing session. We pause before we choose our Quality. Then we reflect on how our writing is going, how we are feeling inside, and what support we need for ourselves. Each student names their Quality out loud and we sit together for a one-minute meditation. Qualities offer support when writing alone or with others.

You can combine Qualities, add adjectives that speak to you, or create your own. A Quality can be any word or phrase that intuitively resonates for you. Here are some recent examples of Qualities students have named in workshops:

- Dedication and Perseverance
- Playfulness and Consistency
- Sense of Calm, Radiant Health

- Consistency and Gentleness
- Unfettered Passion
- Glorious Flow
- Self-Acceptance, Self-Love
- Freedom to Be Creative
- Freedom to Focus on One Thing at a Time
- Sitting with It
- Keep the Flame Burning
- Affirmed
- Freedom to Write What Wants to Be Written
- My Purpose Is to Write This Story
- Bursting through Boundaries
- Patience with Myself
- Hopeful, Bounce Up
- Freshness
- Magic Wand to Trust My Gut

DECK OF QUALITIES

Acceptance	Dream	Hopeful	Pleasing Myself
Affirming	Ease	Humor	Presence
Allowing	Embrace	Imagination	Priority
Appreciation	Empathy	In Deep	Reaching Out
Balance	Energetic Spark	Independence	Reassurance
Boldness	Energy	Inspiration	Reconciliation
Bounce Up	Enthusiasm	Joy	Release and Creativity
Calm	Expansiveness	Joy-Fuel	Resilience
Camaraderie	Family	Joyful	Safety
Change	Feeling Valued	Kindness	Self-Compassion
Choice	Flexibility	Love	Self-Confidence
Clarity	Flow	Magic Wand	Self-Empathy
Comfort	Focus	Momentum	Self-Mastery
Commitment	Forgiveness	Motivation	Shine Your Light
Community	Freedom	Nurturing	Sitting with It
Connection	Freedom to Be Creative	Open to the Lessons	Spiritual Cleansing
Conviction	Freshness	Opportunity	Support
Courage	Fresh Perspective	Order and Structure	Surrender
Creative Expansion	Fresh Start	Passion	The Joy of It
Creative Expression	Gentleness	Patience	Tranquility
Creativity	Gratitude	Peace	Trust
Daring	Grounded	Permission	Understanding
Decisiveness	Growth	Persistence	Unleash
Depth	Honesty	Playfulness	Vulnerability
	Hope		

Chapter Takeaways

- We can choose how we frame our creative struggles.
- Qualities are aspects of our spirit that are always available to support, nurture, and uplift us.
- Choosing a Quality is about summoning support.
- We do not need to justify or make sense of what Quality we chose. It is a uniquely intuitive process.

Exercise: Using the Deck of Qualities

The Deck of Qualities provides a list of creative Qualities so that you can identify and name the Quality that speaks to you as a powerful affirmation of your intention to express yourself. You can anchor to a Quality throughout your writing process. Your Quality serves as a creative life raft for your radical self-expression which can become crucial when doubt and fear creep in.

1. Take a moment to reflect on how you feel when you sit down to write. What obstacles have come up in the past? How do you want to feel inside about your creative process? What kind of support do you wish you had for your radical self-expression? Name what you need right now.

2. Scan the Deck and select the Quality that best matches what you need. Allow your understanding of the Quality

to be enough. You don't need to justify or make sense of why you picked what you picked. Multiple qualities can be selected and combined in any way you choose. You can make a Quality your own by combining Qualities, adding adjectives, or creating a new Quality inspired by your own creativity.

3. Please note you are not limited to Qualities listed in the Deck. The Deck is meant to inspire you and help name what you need. If something else comes up or you are inspired to design a new Quality, that is perfectly acceptable. This is an intuitive process. Allow your heart to be your guide.

4. Build self-support throughout the day, week, month, or forever by writing the Quality down and placing it somewhere where you can see it while you are writing.

5. Before writing, close your eyes, say the Quality out loud, and sit quietly and breathe for one minute. This forces you, the writer, to pause and allow the Quality to come forward. When the minute is complete, you are ready to write.

As you recognize, name, and anchor yourself to a supportive Quality, you continue your liberation from the limiting beliefs that lurk inside.

Exercise: Supercharge Your Quality into an Intention

Naming a Quality provides a powerful support for your desire to express yourself. If you want to take it a step further, you can supercharge your Quality into an intention. Here's how:

1. Use your Quality to craft a statement about what you want to experience while you are writing. For example, if your Quality is Courage, your intention could be, *I am writing with courage and ease,* or *I am a courageous writer.* Do not focus on what you do not want, as in: *I do not want to feel scared when I am writing about difficult situations,* but on what you *do* want: *I am feeling courageous as I allow my words to emerge.*

2. Write your intention as if it is happening right now. If your Quality is Momentum, your intention could be, *I am experiencing joyful momentum as I write.* Do not focus on the future, as in, *I will feel momentum when writing.*

3. Focus on the emotional experience you want to have. Instead of *I have a great writing practice,* use *I am feeling joyful, creative flow as I write.*

4. Avoid words like *try* and use *I am* statements. Instead of *I will try to write at least three times a week,* use *I am writing three times a week with enthusiasm and commitment.*

5. Intentions should be at least halfway believable for the person who creates them. I would not write, *I am always at peace with my self-expression,* because I know I am never *always* at peace. Instead, I would write, *I am supported by the peace that is always inside of me.*

6. Write your intention down and read it as many times a day as needed.

CHAPTER THREE

STEP #3–CREATE A WRITING RITUAL

I remember it was twilight on the day my husband died. The ICU nurse came in to move him from the chair back to his hospital bed. As he lifted him, my husband's legs gave out. I remember the nurse lowered him back to the chair and ran out of the room. I remember my husband managed to raise his head and look at me. I remember how he was adamant that even though he was on the heart transplant list, he would not be leaving the medical center alive. I remember how his eyes locked into mine—knowing his heart was finally done with a long and difficult fight. In nanoseconds, I saw surprise and fear and a beseeching incredulity that felt like he needed me to take care of this. The connection was broken when a horde of doctors and nurses stampeded into his room. I remember someone rushed me out. I remember I let them. I remember how cold the seat of the folding chair was as I sat waiting for the children to arrive. I remember a doctor suddenly appearing, masked, and wearing gloves. I remember praying for the kids to get there.

—Demi N.
Prompt: *I remember*
Timer: 5 minutes

Reduce Anxiety, Increase Confidence

Sometimes when I sit down to write, I think I am surrounded by sunlight, trees, people, dogs, and shoes. I think I am surrounded by coffee brewing, toast toasting, and hands typing, typing, typing . . . But inside there is something else brewing, something that feels suspiciously like doubt and fear. My doubt and fear wear trench coats and think they are cleverly disguised. But I see them. I hear them like carnival barkers beckoning me toward the Ferris wheel. I know who they are. They are ruining my fun, my flow, and my creative spirit. I'm certain I don't want doubt and fear at my carnival. I want snow cones, roller coasters, popcorn, sweet corn, sneakers, and sweatshirts. I want to feel free, adventurous, and bold. I don't want to be turning every corner afraid I am going to bump straight into the things I am trying to avoid. It ruins my mojo, corks up my creativity, and ends with me walking the dog because I don't want to write. This is where a writing ritual can help.

A ritual is commonly thought of as a formal set of repeated acts that serve a function. When we feel afraid or overwhelmed, a ritual can help build confidence and focus. A ritual can be many things, but it does not have to be religious. We ritualize our lives every day. One of my favorite morning rituals is drinking coffee. I choose a mug. I heat up the almond milk. I pour in the coffee. I sit down at my dining room table and look out at the pool while I have my first sip. I need my coffee in the morning but, more than that, I need my morning ritual. My ritual proclaims to all parts of myself—and to everyone in the house—that I am ready to face the day.

You can create a simple ritual to proclaim to all parts of yourself—and everyone in your house—that you are ready to write.

Heart. Soul. Pen. writing workshops begin with a small ritual I call a "palate cleanser." Every class begins the same way: we consider the support we need right now in the moment; we choose a Quality; we name our Quality out loud; we close our eyes and breathe together for one minute; the chime rings; we begin writing.

Research shows that rituals are extremely effective. They can alleviate grief, reduce anxiety, and increase people's confidence when approaching a high intensity effort.[1] For many writers, sitting down to write is a high intensity effort. That is why so many writers throughout history have used rituals and routines to aid their writing practice. Here are examples of a few:

- Stephen King reports, "I have a glass of water or a cup of tea. There's a certain time I sit down, from 8:00 to 8:30, somewhere within that half hour every morning. . . . I have my vitamin pill and my music, sit in the same seat, and the papers are all arranged in the same places. . . . The cumulative purpose of doing these things the same way every day seems to be a way of saying to the mind, you're going to be dreaming soon."[2]

- Elizabeth Gilbert says, "When I'm writing, I tend to go to bed around 9 o'clock. That way I can get up by 4:30 or 5. My favorite time to write is between 5 to 10 a.m., because that way you have the total silence before the world starts chasing you down. By 10 the phone is ringing, emails are coming in, all sorts of things need your care and attention. So I like those secret morning hours. . . . I might write past noon, but that would be rare."[3]

- Margaret Atwood reports, "[In regard to maintaining a regular schedule] I'm a great disappointment in that respect. As a student, I was a night-worker. When I had a child, the writing took place when the child was asleep, which varies during the life of a child. Then when the child goes to school. Then the child goes to university and you revert to some of your former bad habits, such as writing at night. I still do that, but it's a bad habit. You can lose track, and you don't get enough sleep."[4]

- Gillian Flynn says, "I used to stay up until about 3 a.m. writing. That's my natural circadian rhythm. But I've got two kids who I want to see and hang out with in the morning, so I usually get up around 7 a.m. . . . I putter around for a bit, rearrange stacks of papers, clean up the counter. I deliberately don't read or watch anything, because I need my mind clear. Then I sit down and make a list of what I'm going to write that day and what I need to get done on a personal level so I'm not having this worry in the back of my head about what I have to do."[5]

Whether you begin with a cup of coffee or tea, shuffle your papers, light a candle, or simply write at the same time every day or night, you can create your own ritual to help you feel safe, boost your confidence, and get your writing done.

A SPACE OF ONE'S OWN

The first step to consider in creating your writing ritual is privacy. You would be surprised how many students tell me they lack privacy for their writing. They may share the family computer and feel uncomfortable about writing because other people might see it. They may have a desk in the kitchen where their papers and work are not safely protected. It is uncomfortable to bear your soul if your kid, spouse, or roommate is going to make a sandwich and accidentally read it.

Whether it's purchasing a private journal, cleaning up a rarely used spot in the house, or creating an early morning practice while everyone else is sleeping, it is much easier to explore the depths of your heart, take out a shovel and go digging, or allow waves of thoughts and memories and ideas to cascade down upon you when you feel like no one is peeking over your shoulder.

When I was little, my dad had a desk in my parents' bedroom. He would sit at his desk and outline papers in red and do his work. Later, he had a home office where he stored his papers, files, and briefcase. To me, he seemed important. My mom had a desk in the middle of the kitchen with projects and permission slips and calendars stacked on top of each other. She sat at her desk while we made lunches, talked on the telephone, and wrote essays for social studies. My mom tried to keep track of who was going to a birthday party, swimming lessons, or soccer practice while chaos ensured around her.

My mother's space to organize the family was in the middle of everything. My dad had a special space for himself. The message to me was that my dad's work was legitimate. His work was *real.* When he was busy, we had to be quiet. When my mother was on the phone, making appointments, figuring out schedules, or making plans for herself, we were running around talking, eating, and making popcorn in the microwave oven. I got the message that her time and effort was somehow *less important than* my father's. My dad had a space of his own. My mother did not.

During the years that I was a stay-at-home mom, I had a pit in my stomach because I was the one who was not important. I was the one who drove the kids to soccer, swimming, and doctor's appointments. I was the one whose work was not real, at least that is how I felt. These were limiting beliefs that I carried from childhood and came face-to-face with when I became a stay-at-home mother.

Of course, my work maintaining the lives of a family of five was *real work.* And of course, my writing was real work too. I revised and released my limiting beliefs around women's work, but there was reclaiming to be done on the outside as well. I needed to declare my worthiness by taking up space as a woman, a mother, and a writer.

First, I bought myself my own laptop. No longer was I writing on a computer that was used for the kids' school projects, watching YouTube videos, and ordering paper towels from Amazon. My laptop was the first space I claimed for myself. I did not allow anyone else to use it—ever. It was mine and it felt good.

Later, I decided to take over physical space in my house. As the kids got older, I turned their playroom into my office. I added a desk, small couch, and some pillows. Over time, I added objects that spoke to me, like creative talismans. I added a painted tiger statue. I added stacks of beautiful colored pencils. A friend bought me a piece of rose quartz that I placed on a small table with prayer beads and a colorful shawl. Soon, I had created a small shrine to my creativity—a space that held objects that were magical, creative, and made me feel expansive. This space was mine and mine alone.

Creating space for yourself is a statement that you are worthy of carving out room for yourself in your own life—which you are. It doesn't have to be a large space. It doesn't have to be fancy. I had a student who bought a desk and chair and made herself a small writer's studio in the garage. Another student turned an old outdoor shed into her "she-shed," a sanctuary for her writing and creativity. For others, it can be as simple as purchasing a personal journal and special pen or laptop or tablet computer. Creating physical space where your radical self-expression is welcome is an individual endeavor and will look different for each person. Whatever it looks like, making physical space for you acknowledges to yourself that your work is *real,* important, and worthy. In order to create a ritual, you need physical space in which to do it.

There is nothing wrong with enjoying the clatter of dishes, the smell of coffee, and the background noise of bustle when you write. There is no wrong space to choose. It is simply a matter of consciously picking a physical space and making sure that you have privacy. Whether you are at a café or in your car or at your kitchen table in the early hours, if you have space for yourself and privacy, you will feel safer to let your words out.

CREATIVE TALISMANS

A talisman is an object imbued with magical powers meant to protect or heal the person that carries it. Adding a creative talisman to your space is a way to use physical world objects to encourage your creative process. Identifying a creative talisman is an intuitive process. The trick is to open your heart to notice the objects that inspire you. You may decide to go on a walk in nature and see what natural elements jump out. Leaves, rocks, or pinecones may strike your fancy. You may want to visit a metaphysical shop and consider crystals, beads, bowls, candles, incense, or other objects. You can look around your house and identify special pens or pencils, scarves, handkerchiefs, figurines, or family heirlooms to which you are drawn. Consider the sensory details: appearance, texture, shape, scent, sound. A creative talisman is about more than decoration; it is about amplifying your creative experience.

Once you have space and privacy and a talisman, you can begin to create a writing ritual that you use repeatedly when you enter into your creative space. As the ritual becomes second nature, it will help ward away anxiety and resistance. This can be as simple or as elaborate a ritual as you want.

For example: place your talisman nearby, light a candle, name your Quality, and begin writing. Or light incense, close your eyes, do a one-minute meditation, and then begin writing. The point is not to create a writing ritual that is complex, the point is to create a ritual that works for you, that clears away anxiety, doubt, and fear, that helps you connect easily, nearly automatically, to your writing, and that you can repeat each time you face the page.

A NOTE ABOUT TIMING

Sometimes you do everything right. You confront your beliefs. You prepare. You create a ritual and space for yourself. You are ready and yet, still your writing dreams do not materialize. Timing is the hardest thing of all because it is out of your control. Sometimes, things happen, and no matter how carefully laid out your plans are, your writing does not happen. This can be heartbreaking, devastating, and frustrating. What this should not be is an opportunity to beat yourself up. Sometimes situations outside of our control happen and we are presented with an urgent matter that must be handled and we cannot give the love, the heart, the time that we wanted to our writing project.

One writer shared with me a story about how, after careful consideration, she took off a year from her job to focus on her dream of writing a romance novel. She was two months into it when her young son became sick and spent nearly a week in the hospital ICU. She told me that he recovered, but she never did. After this, she simply could not write. Instead, she stayed home and beat herself up mercilessly for not writing and not working. Eventually, she gave up and went back to her job. Six years later, she came to my class. I told her that even though her writing dream had yet to flourish, it was not too late. Not at all.

Too often, writers blame themselves because the book never got written, the essay never got edited, the journal writing fell away, the blog went dark. Timing is everything. Sometimes we show up and the Universe has other plans.

If you tried to launch a writing dream in the past but it was not the right time, forgive yourself and move on. Know that if your writing is calling, you can answer the call. It is not too late. You are not too old. You are not too anything. Your writing is waiting for your attention. Do not use a past disappointment to beat yourself up in the present. Be aware of limiting beliefs! A limiting belief around timing might look like: *I tried this once and I did not succeed so I never will.* This is not true. Consider revising this belief to: *I am in acceptance of the timing of my life. I am answering the creative call now. Now is the perfect time.* We can do everything right and we can still be derailed. Let it go. You are showing up now. Now is enough.

CHAPTER TAKEAWAYS

- A ritual proclaims to all parts of yourself that you are ready to write.

- It is easier to allow ideas to pour out when you feel like no one is peeking over your shoulder.

- Creating physical space for yourself is a statement that you are worthy of carving out room for yourself in your own life—which you are.

EXERCISE: CREATE YOUR OWN WRITING RITUAL

1. Identify a physical space where you can write with privacy. It can be an office, car, garage, shed, closet, kitchen table when everyone is asleep, or bedroom when everyone else is busy. While you are writing, this space is reserved for you.

2. Purchase or repurpose a writing tool (journal, laptop, tablet) that is private and exclusively yours. This tool cannot be shared with others.

3. Collect a creative talisman. Identify an object that resonates for you and name its purpose or significance.

4. Create a ritual or sequence of steps that you can use repeatedly before you begin writing.

5. Write them down in order.

6. Practice your ritual prior to writing to proclaim to all parts of yourself that you are ready to write.

HEART Section Complete:

✓ Step #1—Revise and Release Limiting Beliefs

✓ Step #2—Anchor to a Creative Quality

✓ Step #3—Create a Writing Ritual

PART II

SOUL.

WRITING IS A PROCESS OF DISCOVERY, NOT A CONTEST OF WORTHINESS

When I first returned to writing after a years-long hiatus, I secretly wished for a novel to come pouring out of me. Either that or a polished personal essay, memoir, or some other type of writing that would change someone's life or my own. This was a lot of pressure to bring to my writing. But my career dreams and ambitions had been bottled up for twenty years while I raised kids. Deep inside, there was a small voice of wisdom that told me to let go of the need for more: to be more, to have more, to say more, and just *allow*. Just *be*. But I hated just *being*. I wanted to *accomplish* something.

I brought this need for accomplishment to writing class. It came in my backpack, my laptop, my hands, and in my heart. As I wrote, I could hear my head tell me that my writing was not good enough. That it would never amount to anything and that I should stop wanting so much.

Meanwhile, I felt like a car full of want. Under the seatbelts, in the glove compartment, and every other compartment was my ambition, just waiting to explode when someone popped the trunk. How could I pretend that wasn't true? I wanted my writing to mean something, even though my head kept telling me it never would.

It was as if I had decided that my writing had to *achieve something* to be worth doing. The whole time I was writing, my head was asking: *Where is this going? What is this going to be? What does this writing mean?*

This brings us to the *SOUL* section. Here, we *allow* what wants to be written to come forward onto the page rather than make up words in our mind and put them down on paper. We embrace the concept of radical self-expression, unleashing it from deep inside of us without directing it, degrading it, or needing to know what it is. We move into curiosity and discovery.

Radical self-expression means getting out of our own way so that our words can emerge. It is the opposite of how we viewed writing in school, where we crafted our writing with a thesis statement and three supporting details. There is nothing wrong with this method per se; it is just not how we radically express ourselves and release something that has long been dormant inside of us. My motto is: "Don't think. Just write." This process can be called a "writing dump," "stream of consciousness writing," or "wild writing,'" but it is the process by which we write without thinking or judging.

How do we do this? By writing faster than we think. We don't want to get stuck in our head where judgment reigns. This book is not called *HEAD. SOUL. PEN.* for a reason. The head is the home of judgment. The head tells us to be careful and warns us against humiliation and exposure. The problem with this is that when we are not willing to expose ourselves on the page, we don't allow our truest self-expression to emerge. I believe that what wants to come out—our truest, most radical form of self-expression is not in our heads—it is in our body, soul, groin, chest, pelvis, and under our breastbone. Anywhere but our heads. To dive into soul-centered writing or *radical self-expression*, we don't need to *do* anything except get out of our own way, which sounds easier than it is.

In the *HEART* section, I talked about how I felt when I started to write again in adulthood. I judged what I wrote to be boring, embarrassing, and of little value. These judgments haunted me and made me feel like I should stop writing and be quiet lest I shame myself. I could hear a voice inside of me saying, "Stop wasting your time."

I had an agenda. I wanted to say something "important." I wanted my writing to be "good." I wanted to impress myself and others. Writing about flying from LAX to Fort Lauderdale with three kids while passengers gave me the stink eye hardly felt inspiring. I wasn't able to see that the story was not about travel; it was about motherhood and feeling out of control. My story illuminated an aspect of modern parenting that for me, the writer, was true. But as I typed away, the head kept judging.

There is a saying among writers: *Write what you know.* This is an encouragement to write about subjects, experiences, and feelings with which you are familiar. But what happens when we don't like what we know? When what we know falls into categories that the larger culture tells us are not important? When what we know makes us feel small? When we find ourselves resisting what wants to be written, it is an opportunity to surrender. Surrender does not mean giving up your writing dreams—it means giving up control.

In the *SOUL* section, we dive into writing freely without needing to know where our writing is going and without trying to direct it. We surrender to our radical self-expression. We become curious about our writing. We let our writing tell us what it wants to be.

CHAPTER FOUR

STEP #4—WRITE FASTER THAN YOU THINK

I remember what it used to be like before everyone died. It's sad to think about, I know. But life has been a storm of loss lately, so death and mortality are on my mind 24/7. It's sad to have lost so much in such a short time. First our two cats. Then Grandma. Then our foster kitten. Then my mother-in-law. I am trying not to wait for the other shoe to drop, but it seems the floodgates have opened, and everyone around us continues to pass. But that's just life, isn't it? We're born. We live. We die. It's sad, but I guess it doesn't have to be. Before everyone died, we felt untouchable. Like death was just something far, far away. I wasn't afraid of it. I knew it would come someday, but that day was at least seventy years away. And now that we've lost so many, it feels like death is around every corner. Maybe it is. But that's just death, isn't it? It's sad and it's hard to reckon with, but I guess it doesn't have to be. Grandma's passing was slow and agonizing. My mother-in-law's passing was quick and agonizing. Yet both of them went with grace and peace. Neither went with fear or dread or regrets. And both of them passed with the people who loved them most by their sides. Death is sad, but when you've lived a full life and have people to show for it, I guess it doesn't have to be. So I'll try not to be afraid of dying.

—Cathy T.
Prompt: *I remember*
Timer: 5 minutes

FINDING YOUR VOICE

One of the most common struggles women share with me is that they feel like they have "lost their voice." This makes me think of Ariel in *The Little Mermaid* and how she lost her voice but won the prince. I always thought this story was stupid. Why does the prince fall in love with a woman he does not know and who cannot speak? He does not need to listen, understand, or relate to her because she has no voice. But back to writing.

Losing your voice is no small matter. It is a life crisis, since being content without your voice is nearly impossible. Your voice is your anchor to yourself. When you lose your anchor, you drift aimlessly. Do not wait months, years, or decades to start looking for your voice. Recognizing "I have lost my voice" is difficult because it means accepting that you need to do what it takes to get it back—and soon.

Writing is a great way to reconnect to your voice because it is easily accessible. Writing does not require a new set of sneakers, athletic equipment, or a plane ticket, just paper and pen. Writing will help you connect to who you truly are quickly—it will not take years. Once you start, you will see how little time it takes to find yourself. The key is to take the feeling of "I have lost my voice" seriously and to set aside time to find it.

I work with many women who are also mothers. I like to ask them what is the likelihood that someone is going to approach them and say, "Hey Mom, do you need time for yourself? I thought you might want to skip helping me with that social studies project due tomorrow or forget about making dinner tonight or reschedule taking Grandma to the eye doctor so you can have some writing time for yourself."

If you are waiting for someone else to offer you time to write, you may be waiting a long time. Taking time for yourself is not selfish. It is self-honoring. You are worthy of your own time to connect to your voice, express yourself, and process your world through writing.

HEART WRITING

Free writing or stream-of-consciousness writing techniques are designed to help you write without consciously thinking so that you can access your subconscious thoughts and ideas. With heart writing, we take it up another notch by *first* anchoring to a creative Quality, then writing as fast as we can to a timer until the timer goes off, and letting go of any attachment to what we write about.

Everything about heart writing, from choosing the prompt, to writing as fast as you can to a timer, to consciously cultivating your curiosity, is designed to keep you out of the judgmental mind and into the heart and soul of what wants to be written.

Keys to Heart Writing:

- Anchor to a Quality.
- Write to a timer.

- Write as fast as you can without stopping, editing, or crossing out.
- Consciously let go of having any agenda.
- Choose prompts quickly without overthinking.
- Do not consider prompts prior to writing.
- Avoid getting stuck in the thinking head.
- Allow words to emerge from the heart and soul.

As you know by now, my motto is "Don't think. Just write." In writing classes and workshops, we anchor to a Quality, grab a prompt, set a timer, and write the entire time without stopping. I joke that I am going to move around the room to make sure everyone's pen is moving, or their fingers are typing the entire time. The objective is to stay out of the head and in the heart, soul, and body. I tell students that it does not matter what they write, it just matters *that* they write. When you are in this process, you can write your grocery list, your errands, describe the room you're in, what you are wearing, or your fantasy trip to France. What matters is that you keep writing the entire time, that you write as fast as you can, and that you write without knowing where the writing is going.

Sometimes heart writing feels like you are in an attic sweeping away dust. Sometimes heart writing feels effortless, and when you get used to it, it feels like someone waved a flag and you are off, jumping over hurdles and racing toward the finish line.

Sometimes heart writing feels like you are lost in the woods and there are scary noises all around. Sometimes, as you wander in these woods, you have no idea whether someone is going to jump out at you with a club or if you are going to stumble upon a group of Girl Scouts roasting marshmallows.

With heart writing, you do not know what realms you are going to wander into. That is why you anchor to a Quality and commit to writing until the timer goes off. Otherwise, you might stop because you are scared or unsure where the writing is taking you. You might want to stop to edit, revise, or cross out. But you do not stop because you committed to write the entire time without stopping, so you do.

When the timer goes off, even though I use the "chime" sound on my iPhone, everyone in my workshop jumps. I ask students, "Did the time seem long or short?" Even though many of the students might have seemed terrified when I said we were going to write without stopping for thirty minutes, they inevitably tell me the writing session was too short. They say that they did not get where they were going, or that they were only halfway there, and then chime-chime-chime, it was time to put their pens down.

With heart writing, you allow what wants to be written. You do not have to know what that is. If you keep your fingers moving and your pen skidding across the page, it will come. When you are heart writing, the trick is to get out of your own way.

HOW TO USE WRITING PROMPTS

In *HEART. SOUL. PEN.*, we use writing prompts differently than you may be used to. You may be familiar with using prompts like this: write about a song and a feeling it invoked in you, or recall a childhood memory and tell it from the perspective of your younger self. With *HEART. SOUL. PEN.*, we use prompts in an intuitive fashion, without pre-thinking.

We do not spend time thinking about what we are going to write or how we are going to write about it. We do not spend time considering and selecting writing prompts. Everything about heart writing is designed to push us toward our natural intuition and toward trusting our creative spark. When we choose a prompt(s), we do so quickly, allowing our intuition to be our guide. We tune into what sparks us and grab it to start writing. We trust in the flash of energy we feel as we consider what prompt to use, or we assign ourselves prompts—but we never plan what the story is going to be about, where it is going, or how it is going to come out: poetry, prose, or something else entirely.

What wants to be written already exists inside of you. One could argue that what wants to be written is the same no matter what writing prompt you use but intuitively choosing a writing prompt helps open doors you would otherwise never go through. When you are not thinking, magic happens!

Remember, this is an intuitive process. Simply grab a prompt and go. Do not *think* about it. Do not study it. Do not plan what you are going to write about. Instead, trust your creative spark. Follow the prompt that calls to you. I have provided a list of provocative prompts that have come out of *Heart. Soul. Pen.* workshops at the end of this chapter. If you use these, grab one quickly and start writing.

NOTICE WHAT YOU NOTICE: INTUITIVE PROMPTS

Writing prompts can be found everywhere and anywhere. The most powerful writing prompts are the sights, sounds, smells, objects, lines of dialogue, and images that spark your interest as you walk around your world. Make it a practice to *notice what you notice* and be on the lookout for prompts that naturally ignite your imagination. You may find objects, song lyrics, conversations, or articles that entice you. Capture them, write them down, and then drop the words, images, or objects into your writing.

STRETCH THE TIME

With heart writing, you will notice that the longer you set the timer, the more accustomed you become to writing for that amount of time. So, if you always do a five-minute write, that will become very easy for you. If you always write for twenty minutes, that will become your comfort zone. You can stretch your writing time from five to ten minutes, and from ten to twenty to thirty minutes, by gradually increasing your writing time so that you develop a regular writing practice where you write for thirty minutes a day. More on writing commitments in Step #7—Make and Keep Creative Commitments.

BUILD CONFIDENCE

With heart writing, you become accustomed to approaching a blank page and trusting that your words will come out. In this way, you build confidence in the creative portal inside of you. The more you access your creative portal, the easier it becomes. Your creative portal is always open, even when you think it is closed. You have unlimited creativity inside of you. One good way to keep your words flowing and to avoid corking up your portal with judgment is to remind yourself that your writing does not need to be "good," it just needs to be done. Focusing on writing the whole time without stopping takes the pressure off. Instead of focusing on *what* you are writing, focus on *that* you are writing. This gives your words room to roam and emerge in whatever form they choose.

HEART WRITING DON'TS AND DOS

Don't think your writing needs to make sense. Don't try to redirect your writing to where you want it to go. Don't be disappointed. Don't try to stop your words from meandering into some story you don't want to tell, some secret you don't want to share, or some idea you don't want to have. Don't try to understand what you are writing. Don't allow your mind to judge your writing. Don't try to hide from yourself. Don't beat up on yourself. Do lean into your Quality if you feel scared. Do know that writing is a courageous act. Do acknowledge yourself as courageous. Do believe in your voice. Do celebrate yourself. Do allow your writing to go where it wants to go. Do allow yourself to be free. Do dive jump roll bellow bark beeline fly soar and surf into your self-expression. Do believe you can do this because you can. Do know that your words are worthy because they are. Do use prompts. Do look at your work and wonder at your own creativity. Do let your thoughts, feelings, ideas, and words wander, meander, and tumble out. Do know you are an unlimited fountain of creativity. Do be amazed. Do allow your soul to fly on the wings of radical self-expression. Do know you are worthy of writing because you are.

Chapter Takeaways

- Feeling like you have lost your voice is serious.
- Self-honoring is not selfish.
- You are worthy of your own self-care.
- Heart writing allows you to write without judging everything you write.
- Heart writing is designed to keep you out of the judgmental mind and into the heart and soul of what wants to be written.
- Do not focus on *what* you are writing, focus on *that* you are writing.

Exercise: Heart Writing with Prompts

The purpose of using writing prompts is not to corral your story. It is to give your mind something to focus on while you allow your words to emerge onto the page. The prompt does not matter; what matters is the process: choose a Quality, set a timer, grab a prompt, write without stopping, and see what comes forward. If you write freely and let go of judgment, what is percolating inside of you will emerge no matter the prompt. If you cannot think of a word while writing, just write XX and keep going. You can go back and fill in the word later, but you cannot go back and regain your momentum. Remember: "Don't think. Just write."

1. Decide how long your timed writing session is going to be: five-, ten-, or twenty-minute writing sessions are all good places to start.

2. Grab a writing prompt and use it as the first sentence of your writing.

3. Begin writing quickly without prethinking.

4. Allow the writing to go wherever it wants. The story does not need to be about the prompt. It does not need to have anything to do with prompt. Just use the prompt to kick off the writing session.

5. Start the timer.

6. Write as fast as you can without stopping, editing, or crossing out until the timer goes off.

EXERCISE: COLLECT WRITING PROMPTS

I encourage you to *notice what you notice* and intuitively be on the lookout for writing prompts. When a phrase or line of dialogue jumps out at you, collect it, and drop it into your writing. Do not overthink it; let your intuition be your guide. Of course, there are limitless writing prompts available online. But if you want writing prompts that speak to you, here are simple ways to find lines that resonate for you in your everyday experiences:

- Sit at a busy restaurant or bar and listen for lines of conversation.
- Pay attention to dialogue that sparks your interest as you watch TV.
- Listen for lyrics from songs that speak to you about your own life.
- Be on the lookout for sentences that resonate for you from books, articles, or social media.
- Listen to what people say. Any time you are speaking with another person, a sentence may turn into a writing prompt.
- Pay attention to slogans, quotes, and notes.
- Text messages can turn into great writing prompts.

List of Heart Writing Prompts

The roadies set up mics . . .	The police came . . .
Why couldn't I believe in god?	She took her title of "team leader" way too seriously . . .
We all win . . .	I forgot to lock the door . . .
It was the first time I heard that song . . .	I told her via text I'd be happy to do it . . .
I was beyond obsessed with being skinny . . .	Oh, to be a rock . . .
Would my words ever come out of his mouth?	Should I track her down?
I never did love him . . .	We wore the same cowboy boots . . .
I don't know how long I stood there . . .	I rode my bike home . . .
Should I tell him about the calluses?	No one's hair was dolled up . . .
I assumed it was cool . . .	Try to shrink a gigantic monster into a bottle . . .
I was in an emotional land that had no words . . .	She begged me to leave . . .
Her dad secretly thought I was crazy . . .	I cannot go back to school . . .
Then none of us would be here . . .	Does that make me ignorant?
I was the culprit . . .	I got through the pain . . .
This air quality is concerning . . .	What is wrong with wanting more?
I am debating what to wear . . .	It actually happened to me . . .
I have a new, perimenopausal stomach . . .	We were babies . . .
I need to have yoga blocks . . .	It wasn't personal . . .
I will get to know me again . . .	Love and excitement have to sustain you . . .
I think I like my road . . .	I love the underwear . . .
He is still the one person I text . . .	Can I change?
I will address all of this . . .	I need an extra-wide shoe . . .
All three were divorced . . .	I looked more feminine . . .

That was the third weird thing that happened . . .	She had a headache because she was hungover . . .
There is still time . . .	I only wanted one time to be organized . . .
Darkness has a way of making me hungry . . .	I just have to get out of my bed . . .
Foster kittens are my responsibility . . .	My mom never takes the blame for anything . . .
I imagined worse . . .	We don't want children . . .
There was a man watching me through the window . . .	We don't have enough tickets . . .
I don't remember the first time . . .	She had her chance thirty-seven years ago . . .
My sister did not want to go to the family dance . . .	I have held onto this hurt . . .
I like to develop photos and put them in albums . . .	Whoosh, baby out . . .
I never got a job this way . . .	I was not a loser . . .
My best friend invited me to a psychic medium . . .	When we die, we go back to being air . . .
Why did this affect her?	The world was too silent . . .
He looked at me for way too long . . .	They always say you don't know . . .
It is hard to be an adult . . .	They came back to taunt . . .
Thank goodness I remembered to pack my pill cutter . . .	I was planning an all-nighter . . .
I wore a matching bra and half-slip . . .	I got arrested twenty-two years later . . .
My job is violent . . .	He was the biggest minimizer . . .
I barely set foot in the mall . . .	I much prefer room service . . .
The pencils were everywhere . . .	His rumpled hair entered my room . . .
My aunt taught me to pluck eyebrows . . .	Both of the boys were hardly around . . .
I had aged . . .	Where is she going?
She gently leaned back in a chair . . .	I just can't face it . . .
I will broach the topic with the doctor . . .	Tears. Again . . .
She was supposed to be sleeping . . .	That wasn't the only issue . . .

CHAPTER FIVE

STEP #5—ENTER INTO CURIOSITY AND DISCOVERY

I remember when I found out I was pregnant with my daughter. My husband and I had been intimate one time because life was already hectic with a three-year-old. I recall looking at the calendar and thinking, did I get my period? I couldn't remember because I was laid off from my job and currently looking for a teaching position. But I went down to the store and got a pregnancy test, and my thoughts went wild: There is no way I am pregnant! We can't be pregnant, right? We only did it ONE time. Am I extra fertile? Then I took the test and thought I really have to be overreacting right now. Then I saw the two lines and said, "I don't believe it." Then I got the call for the job interview. The woman on the phone said, "We want to interview you." I made it clear, "Oh you don't want to hire me. I just found out I'm pregnant." She went on to say, "We have resources for you to go on maternity leave. Just come in and see if you are the right fit." So I did. But in my mind, I thought I really don't want this to happen and how am I going to raise two children and be a first-year teacher?

—Dina K.
Prompt: *I remember*
Timer: 5 minutes

RELEASE THE NEED FOR AN AGENDA

Many of us live at warp speed, which, for moms, means living at the speed of kids. In between all the cooking, cleaning, dropping off, picking up, helping with homework, and getting everyone to bed, it's nearly impossible to know how we feel . . . until we sit down and write and find out.

Radical self-expression is the process of liberating your words and releasing them onto the page. Your words are not trapped in your head, mind, or brain, but rather in your body, heart, and soul. Heart writing trains you to get out of the way and let the words flow. But this process can conflict with the role of the head and the thinking mind inside.

The role of the head is to keep us safe and secure. The head wants to protect us from danger, real or perceived. The head judges us in order to protect us so that we will not expose ourselves to humiliation or shame. While we write, the head talks to us and, in its zeal to keep us safe and silent, it creates feelings of doubt and fear which can make us stop writing.

With heart writing, we write as fast as we can to stay in our heart and soul and not get trapped in our head space. But, sometimes, no matter how fast we type or cling to our Quality, we keep hearing the voice that asks, *What is my story? What am I writing? Does this even matter? Where is this going?*

To combat this, we can consciously enter into a state of Curiosity and Discovery (C&D). This alleviates the tension between both wanting to write and wanting to stop writing—at the same time.

Cultivating C&D also pushes us to release having an agenda. Sometimes, no matter how hard we try, the desire to make our writing into "something" gets in the way of radical self-expression.

I was working with a writer who was struggling to finish her second book. During our coaching session, she told me that she kept finding herself going to the grocery store, riding her bicycle, or making travel plans whenever she sat down at her desk. She was not writing. She had completed much of the book, and every time she sat down, she wanted to connect the pieces, drop into the plot, and "get the book done." The more we talked, the more she shared her desire to "finish it." I asked her if she felt like she was pressuring her writing to move her story forward. After some thought, she said, "Yes, because I am."

I know this feeling well. I remember wanting my writing to validate me, to prove to myself I had something to say, to satisfy the ambition inside of me. I also remember how stuck I felt when I approached writing in this manner.

I asked her, "What would happen if you let go of moving your writing project forward and just wrote? What if you were curious about what came out? What if you wrote and simply wondered what you might discover?" Her demeanor instantly changed. She told me she felt like a weight had been lifted.

When we write and bring with us pressure for our writing to "be something," we can short-circuit our creative process. Consciously moving into C&D gives our writing permission to be anything it wants. We become curious about what will emerge, and discover new ideas, thoughts, and words. When we release any need to force our writing into anything other than what it is, writing becomes a tool of curiosity and a process of discovery.

Moving into C& D has three main benefits:

1. Orients the mind away from judgment and toward wonder: instead of the head judging and repeatedly saying, *This is not good. Who will care?* We train our brain to connect to curiosity questions such as, *What is coming forward?* The head is going to talk while you write no matter what. It is easier to listen to, *What is percolating inside?* Rather than, *Does this even matter?*

2. Encourages surrender: C&D requires that we give up planning and instructing and demanding what our writing becomes. It forces us to let go of having an agenda.

3. Releases anxiety: when our writing no longer needs to achieve a goal, we can relax. We no longer need to be anxious about outcomes. We experience more joy and feel lighter.

Enter into the Land of C&D

When women show up at writing workshops and tell me they feel nervous about writing and sharing because they think their writing is not good enough, I tell them we are entering into Curiosity and Discovery, as if it is a real place. In the land of C&D, we do not need to know what we are going to write, and therefore, we let go of the need to perform, impress, or make our writing *be* anything. Here is how we cultivate this mindset:

1. We give ourselves permission to enter into C&D.
2. We consciously welcome all thoughts, ideas, words, and expressions.
3. We focus on curiosity questions such as:

   - What is coming forward?
   - What surprises me?
   - What is percolating inside?

4. We let go of outcomes.
5. We are patient with ourselves.

In C&D, we give ourselves full permission to learn something new, find out something we did not know, and be surprised.

DROP-IN WRITING PROMPTS

One way to encourage moving into C&D is through the use of drop-in writing prompts. Drop-in writing prompts are objects, words, or short phrases that you commit to "drop into" your writing while you write to a timer. Unlike a complete sentence, they are not finished ideas. They are simply words that have no assigned meaning. Drop-in prompts have a two-fold purpose: (1) they force your mind to calculate where and how to include the prompts instead of judging, and (2) they create surprising connections.

Imagine you are writing as fast as you can to a timer, and you have to drop in random words or objects that you selected. This forces you to make surprising choices. Because you are writing as fast as you can without thinking, these decisions are not what you would have consciously chosen, but you do not have time to consciously choose—you just write. This loosening up of the planning mind keeps our creative portal wide open.

Dropping random prompts into your work makes writing feel like a puzzle that has to be solved. You often end up delighted by the way you work the words into your writing. Regardless, this process gives the thinking mind a focus other than judging.

THE RANDOM FIVE

The Random Five is a particularly effective prompt designed to release any agenda for your writing. You choose the first five random objects your eye falls upon and commit to dropping them into your writing. You may think, *I have no idea what a pink sock, a Kleenex box, a rock, a white candle, and a pair of wedge sandals have to do with anything, but fine, I will be curious and see how these items show up in my work.*

The Random Five writing prompt pushes you to relax into curiosity and discovery because your thinking mind has no idea how these items connect, and you do not have time to decide. You have to let go of editing, crossing out, rearranging, and forcing your writing to be something specific. Not only is this fun; afterward, you discover the prompts took you somewhere totally unexpected.

Example: The Random Five

Prompts: pink sock, Kleenex box, rock, white candle, wedge sandals

My pink socks were sitting on the couch in my office. I sit on the couch when I look through my mother's purse. Even though my mom died three years ago, I keep her purse exactly how it was on the night of the fall. When I sit on the floor and remove her leather wallet and Mah Jongg card and her hot pink lipstick and her leopard change purse, I am glad I have a Kleenex box next to me because I cry often and hard. I miss my mother. I prop open the back door to the office with a rock from the garden so that cool air wafts into the room. I find the sound of the pool pump and water falling comforting as I stroke my mom's leather wallet. I know I am crazy to examine all the objects in her purse, but it makes me feel close to her. Sometimes, I light the white candle that sits on the desk and feel the cool air floating in and let myself feel my feelings. Sometimes, I wish I could move fast enough all day and night so that I did not have to feel my feelings, but my grief counselor tells me it is important. After I sit for a while with my tears and my pain and my Kleenex, I get up and put on my wedge sandals and walk my dog. It feels good to get out of the room and out of the house and out

of my head and walk and walk and walk while my dog
sniffs every flower and bush and succulent we walk by.

When I looked back at what I wrote using the Random Five, I was surprised. I did not plan to write about my mom, grief, and loss. Instead, I discovered what was percolating inside of me. When I read my piece, this particular line explained a feeling I had been having but was not aware of: *I wish I could move fast enough all day and night so that I did not have to feel my feelings.*

Moving into C&D opens a whole new world of exploration. In this space, what we write doesn't have to be neat, pretty, groundbreaking, make sense, make other people feel good, move our story along, be an essay, or a blog post. Our writing is not a contest to prove our worthiness. It is an invitation to discover. We get to wonder and be surprised with no attachment to achievement or validation.

Your writing will tell you what it is. You do not need to know what you are writing about or what the writing will *be*; you simply wonder. It is already there inside of you and when you unleash it, you give it the chance to show up on the page. You can read it, relate to it, and slow down enough to feel it, so you do not have to be a stranger to yourself. When you let go and enter the land of C&D, you give yourself full permission to surprise yourself. The joy and the connection are in the surprise. The more you develop the skill of C&D, the more your writing will flow.

CHAPTER TAKEAWAYS

- When you write and bring pressure for your writing to "be something," you can short-circuit your creative process.
- Moving into C&D consciously gives your writing permission to be anything it wants.
- You can train your brain to wonder.
- Your writing is not a contest to prove your worthiness; it is an invitation to discover.
- With C&D, you get to wonder and be surprised with no attachment to achievement or validation.
- Your writing will tell you what it is if you let it.

EXERCISE: COLLECT DROP-IN WRITING PROMPTS

Everyday objects, words, or phrases make great drop-in writing prompts. Unlike a line or sentence, they are not complete ideas. You can collect drop-in writing prompts by attuning to the natural world or by free associating on familiar objects:

- Go outside: Take a walk and collect three objects that intrigue you. You can do this wherever you are: in your neighborhood, on a hike, or in the city. There are rocks, leaves, feathers, and all kinds of tiny natural objects around you. Name them and drop them into a piece of writing. Take a photograph of what you find for inspiration.

- Shoes: Choose a pair of shoes and identify three adjectives that describe them. Put the shoes and the adjectives in your piece.

- Clothing: Look at your apron, bathing suit, slippers, and choose three words or phrases that relate to them. Or go into your closet and choose two items of clothing and have the articles of clothing appear in your writing.

- Photos: Using any image, identify three words that capture what the image says about your life. This can be any picture that strikes you or a photograph you have taken.

- Treasures: Go on a "treasure hunt" in your house and identify three treasures that will appear in your piece.

- Things that are . . . : Choose an adjective and find three things of that ilk. For example, three things that are wild or three things that are sleepy or three things that are scary.

- Name game: List three emotions/three animals/three objects that begin with the same letter as your name and include them in your writing.

EXERCISE: THE RANDOM FIVE WRITING PROMPTS

1. Allow your eyes to look around your space.
2. Write down the first five objects you see. You may use one or two adjectives to describe the object: a yellow

comb, a large hose, a pink sock, a sleeping German Shepherd, a flowered throw pillow.

3. Set your timer and commit to dropping into your writing all five objects. Do not begin the first sentence with one of the five objects; drop them in as you write.

4. Write as fast as you can until the timer goes off and ensure all five objects appear in your piece.

CHAPTER SIX

STEP #6—FOLLOW THE TIDES

I remember when my new therapist told me I was depressed. I said, "No, I'm not." She laughed. And laughed. And laughed. I have been in therapy since I was eighteen years old. I have never had a therapist quite like this one and I have had several therapists over the years. My longest relationship was with a therapist I worked with at my office through the EAP program. She helped me when I got promoted. Then she helped me with my life when I got divorced. She helped me envision what I wanted and once even hypnotized me. I remember the vision—I was standing in a field of tall grasses and there was a yellow sunny haze over the scene. I was wearing a long flowing skirt and I was with a man who was lifting up a little baby with light blonde hair toward the sky. That vision came true. I got married and had a baby. And I was happy. But between the pandemic, menopause, losing a job, selling a house, a close friend passing, financial pressures, and applying to high school for that baby, I became depressed. I didn't realize it though. I stopped painting. I stopped going to yoga. I stopped meditating. When my new therapist stopped laughing, she said, "You are depressed, and I am going to help you come out of it. You are going to buy new art supplies and go to yoga and start meditating again." And you know what? I did all those things and now, nine months later, I can look back and say, that yes, I was depressed, and I can only laugh.

—Dawn G.
Prompt: *I remember*
Timer: 5 minutes

THE TRANSFORMATIONAL NATURE OF STRENGTH-BASED FEEDBACK

How can we understand the power of our work when we read it and immediately notice what is wrong with it?

Have you ever explored tide pools? If you have, you may have had the experience where you touch a sea anemone, and it reflexively closes into itself. People are no different. When your creative tentacles are widespread and flowing and you suddenly get poked hard, your creative portal snaps shut. Your inner arrow drops into a nosedive. Sometimes permanently.

When people shut down your creative process through critique, I call it *art school trauma*. This often happens at school, in workshops, or in writers' groups. This is when you begin writing and are excited about an idea until you receive critical feedback from a teacher, professor, writers' group, colleague, husband, wife, mother or father, and the story that was easily and naturally emerging comes to a screeching halt.

But we do not need other people's criticism to shut down our creative spark. We do it to ourselves all the time. Does this sound familiar: you write something and feel good about it. Maybe you even feel the wind in your hair. Whew! What a ride! But then you read your work and your curiosity and sense of discovery starts to fade. You criticize. You tear apart. You judge your work as *bad* and—poof!—you kill the creative spark behind the flow.

SHIFT YOUR LENS

Strength-based feedback means focusing on the strengths in a piece of writing. It is a supportive process in which you turn your lens toward noticing what is beautiful, mysterious, intriguing, unique, catchy, and interesting in your own work. When you read your writing, you ask yourself: *What strikes me? What do I notice? What moved me? What am I exploring?*

You do not focus on whether the work is *good* or *bad*. Instead, you concentrate on what is present in the writing and how you relate to it.

The founder of Amherst Writers & Artists Method (AMA) Pat Schneider said, "Craft is knowing when to revise a manuscript and when to leave it alone, but art is the fire in the mind that puts the story on the page in the first place."[1]

We want to stoke the flames of the fire in our mind by focusing on what is *at the heart* of our writing, rather than judging it as good vs. bad.

Following the TIDES: Themes, Images, Details, Emotions, and Structure of our work forces us to focus on identifying the elements we notice, rather than fixating on perceived shortcomings. As we turn away from critique, we turn toward connecting to our voice. We find ourselves getting excited to write and writing more, not less. Our arrow points straight up when we are inspired.

Following the TIDES is a guide to sharing strength-based feedback with yourself or with others. Just like you can revise your limiting beliefs, you can shift the lens through which you view your writing. You can choose a lens that supports your goal of connecting to your voice, unleashing your radical self-expression, and seeing the value of what you have to share instead of getting caught in a good vs. bad mindset.

For women, this can be a revelation. We often have trouble seeing the value of our work because we are preprogrammed to believe our value is determined by others. Following the TIDES forces us to turn a strength-based lens onto our own work, instead.

Theme

Writers often tell me, "I don't want to write about my divorce again," or "I don't want to keep writing about my battle with Lyme disease." I tell them it's not about what you want to write; it's about what wants to be written.

The themes that come up in our writing are what concerns us, what percolates inside of us, what we seek to understand and explore. We cannot force our theme. If we are writing about grief, loss, joy, passion, or anger, that is what we are writing about. We are allowed to examine and reexamine our theme—to look at it from every angle—to turn it upside down and right-side up and stare at it in the dark and in dim light and outside in the sunshine. We are allowed to write about the themes that interest us for as long as they interest us. If we try not to, we stick a cork in our self-expression.

Some writers have only one or two themes that interest them throughout a prolific career. It is better to allow the themes to emerge and learn to accept them rather than try to beat them back.

I once had a private client who wanted to write a book on food, but she kept writing about the destruction of her marriage. In other words, her head wanted to write about food, but her heart wanted to express betrayal, endings, and loss. When we want to connect to our voice, attempting to direct or redirect what we are writing about shuts us down. Sometimes, the best we can do is to surrender to what wants to come forward and support ourselves while we do so. I reflected to the client that the book that wanted to be written inside of her appeared to be about loss, not food. Every time she sat down to write, that was the story that emerged.

For a long time, I wrote about losing my mother. Isolated at home during Covid quarantine when my mom died, I did not experience the typical aftermath that grievers face during normal times. There was no funeral, no condolence calls, no food platters from the deli. The traditions and rituals fell away while I suffered a loss in a world where everyone was losing. Three years later, I could barely drive anywhere without yearning to call my mother. When she was alive, I would call her from the car and say, "Hi, Mom." She would ask, "Who is this?" I would say, "Mom, this is the only woman in the world who calls you Mom." And we would both laugh.

Sometimes I did not want to write about losing her. There was too much grief. But when I sat down, that is what came out. I could not make myself *not* write what wanted to be written. Neither can you. I will write about my mother until I am done writing about my mother. You will write about what concerns you until you are done writing about it. The best that you can do is simply honor the themes you notice emerging in your writing.

Images

Images are powerful. Look at your work and notice what images come forward. Was there a lamp in the window? Was there a broken mirror or a solitary shoe or four hundred face masks sitting in a pile on a desk? Noticing the images that come forward in your writing helps draw your attention to the visual and make connections. Again, there is no judgment. We simply notice the images that come forward.

Details

Details bring a piece of writing alive. What details show up in your piece? A little pink pill or a parent's admonishment to "be responsible" or a stick of Trident or peppered whiskers or East Sixty-Sixth Street or a torn hole in a leopard-print sock or $37 or the click clack of heels on hardwood or Pad Thai or corn bread or the smell of eucalyptus? Pay attention to the details in the piece.

Emotions

In a recent writing workshop on processing our pandemic experience through writing, students were surprised by the feelings of hope, connection, and compassion that were present in their writing. They expected darkness, fear, and uncertainty, but many of the pieces focused on the silver linings Covid presented.

Be curious about the emotions expressed in your work and notice them. Sometimes writers in class will apologize and say, "This is dark." Do not apologize. There is nothing bad, wrong, or broken about writing what is dark. Part of our human experience is living in the light and part is living in the dark. It is all worthy of being written about. It is all part of life. You do not have to shy away from darkness or judge it as a downer. You can notice it and be curious about the emotional currents at play in your work. You may notice joy, delight, wistfulness, whimsy, longing, grief, envy, joy, anger, or childlike glee. Rather than judge, simply notice the emotions present in your work.

Structure

As part of our natural writer's voice, our writing comes out with its own unique structure. Again, we don't have to judge the structure of freshly written material. We can simply pay attention to it. Did the piece end where it began? Did it move back and forward in time? Does the work end on a cliffhanger? Notice the structure of your writing and how it begins and ends and whether it ties up neatly in a bow or meanders far afield and then returns.

As you follow the TIDES, you begin to appreciate your own natural writing voice. You notice your details, your humor, your descriptions, and the themes that are important to you. Everyone has a natural writing voice. Yours will flourish when you refrain from judging and focus on the strengths present in your work.

Trigger Lines

To go deeper into your material, after you follow the TIDES of your work, you can hunt for trigger lines in your material. In spiritual psychology, the people and situations that *trigger* us are the ones that bring up issues necessary for our healing. When someone says or does something that makes your blood boil, you have been triggered. Triggers are considered opportunities for growth. So, too, are trigger lines contained in our writing.

Trigger lines in writing are the phrases or sentences that elicit an emotional response and typically begin with "I." These I-lines may not necessarily make our blood boil, but they do strike an emotional chord. When we read our work, trigger lines jump out at us and indicate places where more story is hiding, where there is more to be said, where we have just begun to break the surface. We feel them in the writing. They have energy and call out for further exploration.

Often in workshops, we do a timed writing exercise and then stop and look for trigger lines in our writing. We begin by circling every sentence that begins with *I*. Then we choose the I-line that has the most energy for us and use it as the first sentence for our next timed writing exercise.

This helps us drop deeper into the TIDES of our work. Perhaps the trigger line contains an image we want to further explore or an emotion that has more to say? Using trigger lines to excavate our writing is another way of staying present to the strengths contained in it, the seeds that have been planted, the mysteries that are coming forward, instead of getting into harsh critique that douses our creative spark.

The purpose of following the TIDES and identifying trigger lines is to connect with our voice on the page and avoid—always avoid—allowing ourselves to slip into a judgmental mindset. We want to write more, not less. We want to find our voice, not criticize it. A strength-based lens keeps us curious and open—not disheartened and shut down.

EXAMPLE: FOLLOW THE TIDES AND LOOK FOR TRIGGER LINES

Prompt—If I was able to break those agreements that I made a long time ago . . .

> "If I was able to break those agreements that I made a long time ago, I would," I heard a woman say sitting in the booth behind me. I liked to eavesdrop on people when I was writing because the words and expressions and upsets that people said and shared were so juicy. And sometimes I really needed juice for my writing. It's not like there isn't anything juicy or upsetting or interesting happening in my own life, it is just that I am chronically bored with my own life. That's the truth. I think it's a perimenopausal thing. Restlessness. Itchiness. The sense that something is coming, something good, something big, and I want to just fling myself at it rather than go to Trader Joe's for chicken breasts and

corn if it's in season. I pondered this particular line: *If I was able to break those agreements that I made a long time ago.* What agreements? I wondered what the woman behind me was talking about. I wanted to look at her, but I thought it would be rude to turn my head 180 degrees in her direction. I could try to get a peek out of the corner of my eye, but I could only see a colorful patterned shirt—I could not see her face. What kind of agreements was she talking about? What kind of agreements did she make a long time ago? What kind of agreements did I make? When I think about agreements, I think about marriage. That's an agreement I made a long time ago, but I don't want to break it. Maybe she is talking about deeper internal issues like agreements she made with herself that have to do with self-worth or self-expression or not living too large or keeping herself small. These are the kinds of agreements that women make and they don't even know it.

- Theme—Anticipation, identity, aging, searching for meaning
- Images—The booth in the restaurant, the writer with her ear out listening, a glimpse of a colorful, patterned shirt
- Details—Trader Joe's, chicken breasts, corn, marriage
- Emotions—The restlessness and curiosity of the writer
- Structure—The piece began and ended with agreements. The writer ends up with the question she posed

at the beginning: what agreements do we make in our lives?

Trigger lines—Any of these lines could be pulled out and used as a prompt for the next timed heart writing exercise. I feel more story behind each one:

- I really needed juice for my writing.
- I am chronically bored with my own life.
- I could not see her face.
- I think about marriage.

Chapter Takeaways

- When people shut down your creative process through critique, it is called *art school trauma.*
- Following the TIDES: Themes, Images, Details, Emotions and Structure of our work forces us to focus on identifying the elements we notice rather than fixate on perceived shortcomings.
- As we turn away from critique, we turn toward connecting to our voice.
- Just like you can revise your limiting beliefs, you can change the lens through which you view your writing.
- Women often find it difficult to see their worth because we are preprogrammed to believe it is determined by others.

- Trigger lines in writing are the phrases or sentences that elicit an emotional response and typically begin with "I."

EXERCISE: YOUR TURN: TIDES AND TRIGGER LINES

1. Read a piece of your writing and follow the TIDES:

   - Write down the **T**hemes being explored.
   - Underline any **I**mages that strike you.
   - Circle **D**etails that surprise you.
   - Notice the **E**motions present in the piece.
   - Investigate the **S**tructure: where and how does the piece begin and end? What happens in the middle?

2. Look for trigger lines:

   - Circle lines that begin with "I."
   - Read each I-line and ask yourself if there is more to discover.
   - Circle any other lines that call out to you or have energy.
   - Choose one of those lines as the first line for your next timed writing exercise.

3. Remember your goal is to go deeper into your writing, not to critique.

HEART + SOUL Complete:

✓ Step #1—Revise and Release Limiting Beliefs
✓ Step #2—Anchor to a Creative Quality
✓ Step #3—Create a Writing Ritual
✓ Step #4—Write Faster Than You Think
✓ Step #5—Enter into Curiosity and Discovery
✓ Step #6—Follow the TIDES

PART III

PEN.

THE ONLY PERSON WHO DETERMINES YOUR VALUE IS YOU

As I look back at my writing journey, I cannot remember every essay, journal entry, or blog post I ever wrote, but I do recall how writing changed my life. I felt like I was screaming into the void before I put pen to paper. I had so much to say, and it wanted to come roaring out of me, but it was stuck inside.

I had no creative outlet for my voice. As I have written about in this book, I was a fierce advocate for my kid with ADHD. I would go to the ends of the earth for my child, but those efforts often left me feeling angry, exhausted, and disheartened. Over time, through more situations, incidents, and frustrations, all those feelings festered. I held onto them until I wanted to scream.

When I sat down to write, my heart poured onto the page. I wrote about the time the teacher told my son he would not follow his accommodations and my son told him he had to *by law* and then the teacher sent him to the principal for arguing and the injustice of it all. But instead of my head popping off and spinning around, I wrote the words out of me. Much of this writing later became the basis for personal essays.

Writing connected me to myself, and my voice soared. As I found my voice on the page, I found it in my life as well. It was as if the power of writing began to ooze into my real-world experiences. I became stronger and surer of myself and slowly, very slowly, I stopped caring about what other people thought because I had a job to do: advocate for my kid and write about it. And that was what I did. Later, much of this writing was published.

You are under no obligation to share your story. You do not have to submit, post, or publish your work. Writing will change your life, regardless of what you choose to do with it. For me, becoming a personal essayist was part of my purpose. Who knows what purpose writing will play in your life? For every writer it is different and there is no right or wrong answer.

In the *PEN* section, we consciously consider how we want to move forward *after* we write. Do you want to create a regular writing practice? Receive feedback on your work? Share your writing with others? Submit or post or publish? If so, you can do any or all of it with the same respect for your voice and your value that you have cultivated since Step #1.

In the *PEN* section, we dive into how to create a thriving writing practice. If you choose to share your work, I stress the importance of owning your value and differentiating between outer validation and inner worthiness. How your work is received by any other person on the planet, whether it is your best friend or a literary critic, is not a judgment of your value. The only person who determines your value is you.

CHAPTER SEVEN

STEP #7–MAKE AND KEEP CREATIVE COMMITMENTS

I remember when I used to run. Well, maybe it was more of a jog. I eventually did three miles several times a week. I was in great shape, younger then too. I would wear two sports bras so my double Ds wouldn't bounce all over the place. It helped. I would suit up, depending on the weather. Leggings, T-shirt, sometimes a long sleeve T with hooks for my thumbs so the sleeves covered my hands the slightest bit too. That's for when it was cooler out. I'd put on a baseball hat, my orange one with *Alaska* written on the front, a souvenir from a family cruise years earlier. I'd put in my headphones and listen to music from my little pink iPod nano (I think it was called), motivating me with various beats (Madonna's "Ray of Light," Rage Against the Machine's "Renegades of Funk," Justin Timberlake— anything!, maybe even some One Direction) and I would jog through the neighborhood in a familiar loop. My sister encouraged me, "Just start out a little bit at a time, stop when you need to, push yourself a little more every time you go . . ." and it worked. One of the few times she ever gave me advice that I asked for or listened to when she offered.

—Maya O.
Prompt: *I remember*
Timer: 5 minutes

MAKE IT EASY

"Arrow straight up," my therapist said. "An arrow pointed straight up to the sky is how you feel when you are writing." I knew this was true. I was hiding writing from myself. Not writing regularly was making me miserable.

"I don't eat donuts," my therapist said.

"Why not?" I asked.

"Because I cannot be myself when I eat donuts," she said. "It is that simple, and for you," and she pointed at me with her pink fingernail, "you need to write. Writing for you is a must. Some people have to avoid things and some people have to do things. I cannot eat donuts. You have to write."

We were talking on Facetime, she in her home office and me in mine. And she was right. I did not feel connected to myself when I did not write. I had been in a great writing groove and then my mother got sick. As she got worse, I stopped writing. After she passed away, I struggled to get words on the page. I wanted to write. But instead, I was eating donuts.

Writer self-sabotage is a real thing. Sometimes it occurs when our writing is uncomfortable. Sometimes it happens when we fall out of our creative flow. And sometimes it happens because we get discouraged. I know if I want my life to feel like an arrow up, like an arrow pointed in the direction of joy and creativity, then I have to commit to my writing and get it done. I can talk about how busy I am, how I have no time, and a million other excuses and distractions, but the success of a regular writing practice is less about how much writing you get done, and more about how you approach your commitment to writing.

When we want to write but find ourselves unable to, it may be that the material coming up is disturbing. If you feel like you are circling a subject in your writing, it is important not to beat yourself up. Instead, simply respect your inner fears.

Not being able to write can also be due to making commitments that are not in alignment with your time and energy. You overcommit and then do not write and then blame yourself for not writing, instead of making your writing commitment smaller and easier to achieve.

Do not hold your writing against yourself. Do not use your writing commitment as a way to prove you are not good enough. Do not get in the habit of making writing commitments that you know you will not achieve. Be kind to yourself. Make your writing practice easy. Be willing to course correct if you are not able to get your writing done when you commit to it.

DERAILMENT

Here are examples of how our best intentions get derailed:

Scenario #1

Intention: I am going to write today. I drive the kids to school, grocery shop, walk the dog, scroll social media, answer text messages, drop off an Amazon package, make dinner, help with homework, do laundry, bathe kids, get kids to bed, collapse. Result: I did not write today.

Scenario #2

Intention: I am going to write today. I go to work, go to the gym, shower, scroll social media, make dinner, answer emails, watch Netflix, collapse in bed. Result: I did not write today.

Scenario #3

Intention: I am going to write today. I post on Instagram, send emails, pull up a document, stare at the document, answer the phone, scroll social media, order new pens on Amazon, visit author sites on Facebook, look at the document again, make dinner, read the news, think about writing, collapse in bed. Result: I did not write today.

Do any of these scenarios feel familiar?

There is no better time to distract ourselves than when we say we are going to write. Suddenly, we need to clean out the garage, go through the closet, pay bills, or do writer-adjacent activities, like visit a Facebook writing community, buy a writer domain name, or read publishing industry news. We can keep the day so full that by the time we collapse in bed, we never got to our writing.

This is not unusual. Whether it is because the material coming up is difficult, finding time is tough, or for any number of other reasons, if you find you are not writing and you want to write, consider making your writing commitment so small you cannot fail.

DON'T LET THE SMALL BE THE ENEMY OF THE DONE

Imagine a ladder with rungs that are eight feet apart. It would be impossible to climb from rung to rung.

Now imagine a ladder with rungs that are eight inches apart. It would be easy to climb up that ladder, one foot over another. Why place the rungs eight feet apart when no matter how much you stretch, pull, and kick your leg over your head, you won't be able to climb up?

Make it easy. Ask yourself, *What is an eight-inch rung for me?* Is it writing for ten minutes once a week? Is it writing for twenty minutes twice a week? Set the rungs so close together that the climbing is easy. Do not make it hard!

If you think that a small commitment to writing is not worth making because it is too tiny to matter, this is not true. In fact, that line of thinking is a limiting belief, one that sounds like, "If I cannot write for X hours every day than it is not worth writing." Recognize this is false. Making a very small commitment—even five minutes three times a week—can be an effective way to begin a regular writing practice.

COMMIT

Consider that if you committed to writing five minutes three times a week, in one year, you will have written for 780 minutes. That is 780 minutes more than you would have written if you dedicated zero minutes each week to writing. After one year, you will have made and kept your writing commitment to yourself 156 times. This success builds a trust relationship with your creative self.

A commitment is not a *maybe* or a *might*. It is establishing with certainty that you will complete a task. If writing for five minutes three times a week is an eight-inch rung for you—it is easy and doable—then this is a great place to start.

As the weeks and months go by, you can always increase your commitment. If you successfully write for five minutes three times a week for months, push it to ten minutes or to four times a week. Grow your practice, rung by rung until you settle into a regular writing routine that works for you. Success builds upon success. Keep your rungs small and gently move them further apart until your ladder is the perfect combination of doable, easy, and effective—this will be different for every person. I have a student who writes for three hours five days a week and another who writes for twenty minutes twice a week. Both have happily settled into writing regularly.

Often when you make small, easy-to-achieve commitments, you find that your five minutes of writing time turns into forty. You can always write more than you commit to, but once you have fulfilled your time commitment, you have achieved your goal. The rest is a bonus. It is much better to make small commitments and exceed them, than make large ones and fail to reach your goal.

GET TO KNOW YOUR NATURAL CREATIVE INCLINATIONS

When you commit to a weekly writing practice, you get to know your natural creative inclinations. Do you like to write in the morning, afternoon, or night? Do you prefer to sit in your office, bedroom, kitchen table, porch, coffee shop, or library? Tune into your natural creative impulses. If you find writing in the morning works best, do not plan to write at night before bed when you are tired. Discover when your creativity is at its highest point.

If you do not know when or where you feel most creative, experiment. Try writing in different places at different times and see when and where you have the most flow and what feels best and easiest. You are looking for the sweet spot where writing feels good and effortless; you are not trying to force yourself to write through mud.

Remember: you are practicing making and keeping creative commitments to yourself, not making things hard and difficult. You are practicing reinforcing your wins, not beating yourself up for your losses. You are leaning into what works for you, not trying to dictate what you want to work and then being mad when it doesn't. You are building trust when it comes to writing so that you know when you commit to write, you do it.

COURSE CORRECTIONS ARE GOOD

If you are not getting your writing done, be willing to change course in a way that is supportive and kind to yourself.

For me, it is about getting into the flow. I tiptoe around writing until I get into a regular pattern. When I experiment and find the sweet spot at that moment of my life, I have momentum and am able to stick to a schedule of writing. It may take several tries of stopping and starting until I figure out what works for me.

Making and keeping creative commitments is not a race or a competition. You are not judged by how much time you write, or compared against how much time other people devote to their writing. The commitment you make is to *yourself* to keep up *your* momentum based on the factors of *your* life. The commitments you make are minimums; you can always write for longer periods of time or more often. But once you complete the time you have allotted, you have kept your commitment.

CELEBRATING YOURSELF IS HARD AND CRITICAL

I invite women at writing workshops to celebrate themselves for showing up, which is nine-tenths of the battle. It can be especially difficult when there is a part of you that feels like writing might be uncomfortable, intimidating, or scary. The bottom line is simply showing up for yourself is worthy of being celebrated.

Writing is a process that takes time and effort. It is important to find moments to acknowledge yourself and celebrate your effort. As part of your writing ritual, you can acknowledge your courage. You can celebrate making time for self-expression when you sit down to write in your journal. You can acknowledge that writing is a form of self-care and a gift you give to yourself. Recognizing your hard work and your commitment may sound easy. But, for many women, it is outside their comfort zone. Be willing to experiment with incorporating self-acknowledgement into your writing practice. You deserve it.

Chapter Takeaways

- Do not let the small be the enemy of the done.
- Ask yourself, *What is an eight-inch rung for me?*
- Success builds a trust relationship with your creative self.
- Keep your rungs small and gently move them further apart until your ladder is the perfect combination of doable and easy and effective.
- It is much better to make a small commitment and exceed it, then make a large one and set yourself up to fail.
- Lean into your natural inclinations to discover when your creativity is at its highest point.
- Showing up is worthy of being celebrated.

EXERCISE: CREATING A REGULAR WRITING PRACTICE

Imagine your creative commitments as rungs on a ladder. You want to make achieving your commitments easy. You want to hop from rung to rung with a sense of accomplishment. You want to set yourself up for success. What is an eight-inch rung for you? Is it writing twice a week for ten minutes? Is it writing three times for twenty minutes? Set the rungs so close together that the climbing is easy.

1. Consider your life, schedule, routines, and desires and choose a writing commitment. Make sure it is small enough that you cannot not do it!

2. Ask yourself, *Does this seem realistic? Does this seem doable? Does this seem easy?*

3. Schedule your writing time in your calendar.

4. At the end of the week, review your writing commitments. If achieved, celebrate yourself and repeat. If not achieved, course correct. Go back to #1 and choose a smaller, easier commitment.

5. Remember: do not be afraid that your commitment is too small. The point is not how much you write; the point is *that* you write. This is not a contest. Connecting to your voice on a regular basis keeps your creativity flowing.

CHAPTER EIGHT

STEP #8–SHARE WITH INTENTION

I remember the feel of the hot tea and its sweetness as it ran down my throat and straight into my bloodstream, the taste of the tuna sandwich, its substance the equivalent in that moment of a full roast beef dinner with all the trimmings, including a Yorkshire pudding covered in gravy. The nurses had covered me in a warm blanket, the blood covering the floor just to the side of the bed had come from my body only thirty minutes earlier. I didn't look now, but I remembered watching the midwife tug on the umbilical cord after the baby had finally been born. She was frantic because my body, exhausted, would not expel the placenta. Then the blood came, and the doctor pushed me back onto the bed and inserted a drug to induce my body, unwilling, to release the baby's empty home from my uterus before it could kill me. A tiredness was settling into me that would last for months. It hadn't been until I was given a catheter to drain my bladder that the hours of pushing led to the immediate swoosh of the baby down the birth canal and out of my body and into his father's hands. I knew I should be happy, relieved, elated, but I was overwhelmed. I focused on the sweet tea and sandwich, the very best meal I have ever eaten in my life.

—Lisa H.
Prompt: *I remember*
Timer: 5 minutes

Understand Discernment: Writing Does Not Equal Sharing

As you know by now, my writing motto is, "Don't think. Just write." I encourage you to let your fingers fly across the page without knowing what is coming forth and let the words, thoughts, and ideas emerge from your heart, soul, and gut and get them onto the page. Then, look at the strengths, follow the TIDES, and explore the trigger lines where you can go deeper. When the writing is done and you surface from the depths of your creativity, that is the time you might wonder, what is next? What is my intention with my writing?

The first thing to remember when it comes to sharing your work is that writing does not equal sharing. You will not write a poem and find it posted on your Facebook page unless you post it. You will not read your personal essay in *The Washington Post* unless you pitch it. Your work will not suddenly be available as a memoir unless you publish it. There is wall between the writing process and sharing your work and that wall is called discernment.

Writing >>> Discernment >>> Sharing

Discernment is the space between writing and sharing where you stop and consider the next steps you want to take with your writing. It is the process by which your thinking mind considers the possible outcomes of sharing your work in the world and makes decisions about privacy, timing, and consequences.

In the discernment phase, you ask yourself questions like:

- What does this writing want to become?
- Have I written this for myself or for others?
- What do I want from this piece of writing?
- With whom do I want to share it?
- Is now the right time to share it?

To understand your intentions with your writing, you stop and consider the following:

- Privacy: Is this writing private, or do I want to share it? If so, do I want to share it widely or with a specific person or group?
- Timing: Is this the right time to share this piece of writing?
- Possible outcomes: How will sharing my writing affect me? How will sharing my writing affect others, e.g., my family, friends, career? Am I okay with the possible outcomes?

The discernment phase is a distinct space between writing and sharing.

It is important to remember that discernment is a separate process between writing and sharing because when you conflate the two, you can become paralyzed, worrying that what you write might hurt, disparage, or upset another person. You cannot write freely when you think other people will have access to your work. You decide if, with whom, and when to share your writing during the discernment process.

I bring this up because it inevitably arises during the writing process. You might suddenly freeze and think, *what if someone reads this? What will people think?*

When this happens, I like to remind myself that this is fear talking. My writing is for me alone. Your writing is for you alone. You are not committing to sharing your work by writing it. Your writing is private unless you decide otherwise. In order to write freely, it helps to remind yourself that there is a discernment phase, after writing and before sharing, where you consciously decide what next steps, if any, you want to take with your writing.

Knowing that the discernment process comes after writing and before sharing helps give you the full permission you need to write freely without censoring yourself.

WITH DISCERNMENT, THERE IS NO RIGHT OR WRONG DECISION

When writing, particularly about difficult subjects, it is important to allow your story to come forward onto the page. After that, you can make a decision about whether or not to share your work.

The first part of the process is writing freely and allowing what wants to be written to emerge. The second part is discernment, where you, the writer, consider privacy, timing, consequences, and what next steps, if any, you want to take with your writing. When it comes to sharing your work, there is no right or wrong decision. It is up to you to determine what you want to do with your writing. For some writers, sharing their work is crucial. For others, the act of writing the story and letting it emerge is enough. It depends on the writer and what they are writing about.

One writer I worked with initially thought she would fictionalize her story. She changed the names and details of characters and began to write her book as fiction only to discover that she needed to claim her experience and, eventually, she wrote a memoir. As she considered how and why she wanted to share her story and what the possible consequences could be, she spent time in the discernment phase.

Another writer found herself writing about the harassment she experienced in her early life. She wrote freely, but when she entered the discernment phase, she felt complete with the writing, having unleashed the story from her heart and body. This was enough for her. There are no right or wrong answers to the questions that arise in discernment. There is just what feels right for you.

When we slip into believing: *If I write this, everyone will know or my family will be angry* or *I will have to defend myself,* we need to remind ourselves that discernment is the wall of separation between writing and sharing. You do not have to share everything you write. You do not have to share anything you write. There is an impenetrable wall between writing and sharing. Your words will not leak out unless you make the decision to release them. When fear of exposure threatens your ability to write, remind yourself that, after writing freely, you will enter a discernment phase where you consciously decide whether to share your work or not.

Asking Others for Feedback

When asking for feedback on emerging material, you want the feedback to enhance your confidence and inspire you to dig deeper. Emphasizing what is working in your writing builds enthusiasm and momentum. If feedback causes you to stop writing, it is the wrong kind of feedback. Remember: you are the expert of your story.

I spoke about art school trauma earlier in this book. Feedback that shuts you down is not helpful; it disconnects you from your creative portal. It disheartens you. It makes you feel like you cannot write. But you can.

One student told me that she was working on a short story and sent it to her mother. Her mother offered critique. When the student tried to return to writing the story, all she could think about was her mom's comments. She lost enthusiasm for the story and abandoned it. The point is not that her mother was wrong; the point is that the writer was not ready for feedback. The story was just emerging.

Another student wrote a first draft of a personal essay and sent it to a former writing teacher who edited it extensively. The student never finished the essay because the feedback confused her, and she lost the thread of what she wanted to say.

When you are inspired or curious about a story or idea that is emerging, interrupting your creative process to ask other people what they think about your work is not helpful.

Take the emerging idea as far as you can before asking for critical feedback from others. Remember: you are the expert of your story.

For freshly emerging material, the most helpful feedback is strength-based feedback. A reader can follow the TIDES and share with you what they noticed about the Themes, Images, Details, Emotions, or Structure of the piece. They can share where they would like to know more. That's it. No red lines, no crossing out, no extensive notes or comments or revisions. Strength-based feedback is all you need with new material. We will practice following the TIDES in other writers' work more extensively in *HEART. SOUL. PEN. In Action* (see part IV).

LET YOUR CAKE BAKE

Think of writing your story like baking a cake. Imagine you are in the kitchen with a white apron tied around your waist. You have poured flour, sugar, butter, and eggs in a big silver bowl, and you are mixing it by hand. After you have been stirring your little heart out, you pour the cake batter into a baking pan and then a friend walks in. She looks into your pan and says, "This is not a good cake. It is lumpy. It will not hold its shape. This cake is terrible. It won't taste good."

You stand there in your apron with flour smudges on your black pants and a spatula in one hand, staring into your cake pan. You found the recipe, went to the market for ingredients, mixed, stirred, and poured, enjoying every second, and before you have even placed your cake into the oven, you are completely discouraged. Your cake is no good. You know this is true because your friend told you so.

Is your friend a professional baker? Has she baked hundreds of cakes before? Either way, who cares? If she says your cake is not good, then it must not be. Even if she is not a professional and has never baked a cake in her life, still, she has seen cakes. She has tasted them. And she knows your cake does not look good. You hang up your apron and throw your cake in the trash.

This is what we do with our writing.

We forget the cake was not baked. We did not even get the pan in the oven. We did not need a pastry chef, friend, or anyone else to comment on our cake. What we needed was to let it bake, remove it from the oven, and let it cool. Was it a birthday cake or did we want to write *Congratulations* on it in big red letters? Were we going to add pink roses or vanilla icing or douse it in sprinkles? We will never know because we threw it in the trash!

Do not invite other people into your creative process before your cake bakes. Let your writing emerge and become what it wants to be. Have patience. Ask for strength-based feedback. Revisit, revise, and dig until you, the expert of the story, feel finished. Then you can ask for critique and, even then, be careful to protect your creative portal so that you do not allow art school trauma to shut you down.

HOW STRENGTH-BASED FEEDBACK WORKS

Back to the cake scenario: what if you were standing in the kitchen in your apron baking a cake and your friend walked in and said, "I noticed how smooth and well stirred the batter is," or "I like your idea of adding walnuts and chocolate chips to the mix," or "The smell reminds me of my grandmother's kitchen," or "I wonder what type of cake this is and who you are baking it for?" or even, "I find your baking comforting because it reminds me of how my sister and I used to bake cakes in my first apartment."

Can you see that this type of feedback respects that you are the expert of the cake? It acknowledges the baking process and offers questions. In this scenario, when your friend leaves the kitchen, I doubt you will feel like throwing your cake in the trash. This is the power of strength-based feedback. It is helpful, encouraging, and thought-provoking, not hurtful or destructive or counterproductive.

YOUR JOB IS TO PROTECT YOUR CAKE

Be attuned to how you feel. It is your job to protect your cake and nurture your creative spark. If you take a writing workshop and the class makes you want to give up writing, consider taking a different workshop. When you receive notes that are strength-based, you should feel excited to dig back in and get to work. If you receive feedback that makes you want to give up, the problem is the feedback, not the writing.

CHAPTER TAKEAWAYS

- Writing does not equal sharing.
- Discernment is the space between writing and sharing where we consider our options and make decisions about the next steps we want to take with our writing.
- Your writing is private unless and until you decide otherwise.
- You do not have to share everything you write. You do not have to share anything you write.
- When you are inspired or curious about a story or idea that is emerging, interrupting your creative process to ask other people what they think about your work is not helpful.
- Be attuned to how you feel.
- Freshly written material is not ready for critique.
- If feedback causes you to want to write less, it is the wrong kind of feedback.
- You are the expert of your story.

EXERCISE: HOW TO CONSCIOUSLY ASK FOR FEEDBACK

1. Allow your writing to emerge.
2. Identify trigger lines and go deeper.
3. Ask for strength-based feedback. Follow the TIDES and ask what Themes, Images Details, Emotions, and

Structure struck the reader about your writing and where they wanted to know more.

4. Go back into your piece and edit, revise, and dig deeper.

5. Take the piece as far as you can on your own then consider asking for critique.

6. When asking for critique, set specific expectations: what you are asking for? A simple acknowledgment of your hard work? A full edit with detailed notes and revisions? Notes on structure only? Line edits on grammar and punctuation? Be sure you and your editor understand what you are asking for.

CHAPTER NINE

STEP #9–OWN YOUR WORTHINESS

I remember the feel of my grandmother's soft velvety cheek. The way it felt against mine as she held my head between her hands and pulled me in to kiss my cheek and then rest hers against mine. The smell of her Jean Nate body soap that enveloped me in her embrace. She had sparkling blue eyes and wore her salt and pepper hair in two long braids that she crossed over the top of her head and were held in place with tortoise shell hair pins. She was not a big woman, maybe 5'4" at the most, and yet, she gave birth to 6 giants, all boys and all over 6 feet tall. My own father topped them all at 6'7". She was born in the Netherlands in 1901. As a young woman, she met my grandfather while working as a chemist for Phillips. He was a widow nearly twenty years her senior having lost his wife in childbirth and now was a single father raising his daughter alone. They lived and raised their boys in the Netherlands until 1936 when my grandfather, fearing the rise of Hitler, decided to leave everything behind and move his family to the United States.

—Rianna B.
Prompt: *I remember*
Timer: 5 minutes

External Validation Is Fun But It Is Not the Truth

After I started to publish my work and had more confidence in what I wrote, I felt like "a writer." I no longer felt embarrassed when people asked me what I did. I would say, "I am a writer." And I meant it. In fact, I remember talking to a friend of a friend who asked me about my writing. He said, "You are a self-taught writer, correct?" I wondered what he meant by that question. What does self-taught even mean? Mrs. Schmidt taught me to write in first grade. Books taught me how to make stories and college courses and two graduate-degree programs provided plenty of writing practice. But perhaps I am "self-taught"? In a way, aren't we all? I just smiled and nodded yes.

With my newfound, self-proclaimed title of "writer," I sent out my work and pitched essays to editors. Sometimes they were accepted and other times they were not. There were stretches of weeks or months when I would pitch essays, and nothing would get accepted. Of course, I'd get frustrated with my writing, even though that is not why I was writing in the first place. I realized that I could not let other people determine the value of my work. I knew that it was not the job of my writing to validate me. Art is a fickle gig. You can send out your work and no editor wants it. Then, after what feels like a hundred rejections, you end up placing something in a dream outlet. It happens all the time. Does that change your value? No. Does it change how worthy your writing is? Not at all.

While external validation is fun—and sometimes thrilling—it is not the truth.

The truth is that you are worthy, your story is important, and your voice matters. It is important to separate your inherent value from unpredictable external validation. Do not mix the two. When you do, you can become discouraged and stop writing. In order to support your vibrant writing practice and encourage the unleashing of your radical self-expression, remember that external validation is not a reliable indicator of value. Sometimes you will hear high praise from people who love your writing. And sometimes, crickets.

Either way, keep writing. Keep writing because *you* need your voice. Keep writing because writing makes *you* happier, more at peace, less stressed, and more like yourself. Keep writing because your writing is important to *you*. That is enough of a reason to do it.

If you share your work, know that the response to your writing is not a judgment of the value of your work. Your value is inherent. Remember the ten truths from the beginning of this book? Here they are again:

Ten Truths You Need to Know about Yourself as a Writer

1. You are enough.

2. What you have to say is enough.

3. Whatever you have to give is enough.

4. Whatever time you have is enough.

5. Your voice is unique.

6. Your story matters.

7. You are the only one who can tell your story.

8. Now is the perfect time.

9. You have everything you need.

10. Writers write. If you are writing, you are a writer.

DETERMINE YOUR POINT OF ACTION

Your job is to show up on the page, write from the heart, unleash your words, and know that what you say has value. That is your job. You have the tools to do it. It is not your job to make outcomes happen. You are not capable of controlling outcomes. Your job is to put your energy into writing and, if you wish to share your work, send it out and see what happens.

You do not determine whether your essay gets published or goes viral. Or whether an agent offers representation or sells your book or novel. It is your job to do the work, not determine the outcome. You cannot determine the outcome no matter how hard you try—and trying to control outcomes over which you have no control will make you disheartened, disappointed, and possibly miserable.

When I find myself getting crazy about external forces, I consider all the concerns, worries, hopes, tasks, and dreams I have for my work and place them in one of two columns: *What I Can Control* vs. *What I Cannot Control.*

Under the *What I Can Control* column, I put writing, pitching, posting, research, social media. I track the actions I take toward my writing goals.

Under the *What I Cannot Control* column goes all the outcomes that are not under my control: getting an essay accepted, having readers post nice comments, signing a book deal, getting an agent, or any other outcome over which I have no control. If I am focused on the *What I Cannot Control* column, then I redirect my attention to the *What I Can Control* column because that is the point of action where I have agency.

Here is an example:

What I Can Control	What I Cannot Control
Writing daily	Getting an essay published
Pitching an editor	Going viral
Posting on social media	Securing an agent
Sending a query letter to an agent	Receiving praise from colleagues
Spending time doing research	Selling a book proposal
Drafting a book proposal	Winning a poetry award
Submitting a poem	Selling a novel
Working on a novel	Getting good reviews
Posting on my blog	Becoming a bestselling author
Revising my limiting beliefs	Gaining social media followers
Anchoring to a Quality	Getting a book optioned
Using strength-based feedback	Having an article syndicated
Sharing with intention	Becoming famous
Keeping my creative commitments	Receiving external validation as a writer

When you look at the two columns, you decide what your writing life is going to look like by working in the *What I Can Control* column. You control engaging in a nurturing relationship with yourself, your writing, and your worthiness. You control how much time you spend writing, researching, or working. You do not control outcomes. You do not control whether or not you receive external validation. You do the work that you feel called to do and then you let it go.

Your value is not something you should give away to any other person, entity, or organization. If you do, you will fall into the limiting belief that the outside world determines your worth. Then, if your writing does not deliver the hoped-for results, it will be easy to think it does not have value. This is not true.

CHAPTER TAKEAWAYS

- Art is a fickle gig.
- Your job is to show up on the page.
- Your job is not to make outcomes happen.
- Focusing on *What I Can Control* is where you have agency.
- You do not control whether you receive external validation.
- Nothing outside of you determines your value.

EXERCISE: CREATE CONTROL COLUMNS

1. Draw a line down a piece of paper and form two columns. Label them *What I Can Control* and *What I Cannot Control.*

2. Write down your concerns and worries and hopes and tasks.

3. Determine which column they go in and place them appropriately. Place your tasks under the *What I Can Control* column (writing, pitching, submitting). Place outcomes over which you have no control under the *What I Cannot Control* column (winning awards, having work published).

4. Determine your point of action.

5. If there are steps to take under *What I Can Control*, take them.

6. If your attention is focused on the *What I Cannot Control* column, redirect your attention, release concerns, and let go.

HEART + *SOUL* + *PEN* Complete:

✓ Step #1—Revise and Release Limiting Beliefs

✓ Step #2—Anchor to a Creative Quality

✓ Step #3—Create a Writing Ritual

✓ Step #4—Write Faster Than You Think

✓ Step #5—Enter Curiosity and Discovery

✓ Step #6—Follow the TIDES

✓ Step #7—Make and Keep Creative Commitments

✓ Step #8—Share with Intention

✓ Step #9—Own Your Worthiness

Next Stop: Step #10—Receive the Divine Download

CHAPTER TEN

STEP #10—RECEIVE THE DIVINE DOWNLOAD

I remember that the pressure in my sinuses makes me want to lie down and there is something in my jack-o-lantern stretch pants that is poking into my inner thigh and these two sensations are causing me severe distress. There are these damn mosquitoes, and they swirl around my head as I do my Peloton workout and make me anxious in my downward dog and I reach and clap and try to squish them between my hands and make a loud clapping sound which startles the dog. I remember to eat lunch with my dad and my brother and my stepdad. I told my husband that if he and my son had been at the restaurant then every single important man in my life would have been present. We ate chips and salsa, although I did not eat chips and salsa because I make it a rule not to eat chips and salsa or French fries or donuts or cheap birthday cake at kids' parties. These rules used to work, and I was able to maintain a reasonable weight and fit into my mom jeans, but something has happened in the past year or so and the flesh has gathered around my middle. While my face still looks normal in pictures, the jeans do not fit and that's why I wear festive leggings and try to divert people's attention away from my midsection by tying a jean jacket or sweatshirt around my waist. But this strategy does not work and only makes me look slovenly.

—Missy D.
Prompt: *I remember*
Timer: 5 minutes

WHAT HAPPENED WHEN THE DIVINE DOWNLOAD HIT ME (AND IT'S COMING FOR YOU!)

When I started to write again after years of not writing, I took a weekly writing class. Then I made a commitment to write three times a week for twenty minutes. Soon my twenty minutes turned into thirty and the thirty minutes turned into two hours. I started waking up, feeding my kids breakfast, dropping them off at school, coming home, and writing all day until it was after 2 p.m. and I had to pick them up.

I did not get dressed. I did not eat lunch. I did not get the mail. I did not do anything but write. It was like something happened to me. I could not stop writing. I wrote and wrote and wrote. I did not answer emails, text messages, or go to the grocery store. I just wrote.

I was halfway through a novel before I realized I was writing a novel. Thank God because if I had known I was writing a novel, I never would have let myself.

As I wrote, I laughed, cried, stopped and bit my nails, and worried about what was going to happen to my protagonist. I did not write the story in chronological order, so the plotline was somewhat confusing. Was she emailing her boyfriend from college? Did her husband know? What did her best friend think? I just kept following the energy and writing.

When I was driving, on more than one occasion, I had to pull over and dictate dialogue into the Notes app on my iPhone because suddenly whole conversations were coming forward.

When I took my kids to soccer practice, I wrote in my car. When we were on a flight to Florida, I wrote between setting up movies and headphones and bags of chips for the kids.

I wrote before dinner and after dinner. At one point, my youngest asked me if I loved my laptop more than them. That forced me to take a break and give my kid some TLC. But the story just wouldn't stop. It came flying out and I had to keep my fingers on the keyboard to translate. Nothing like this had ever happened before. I never once wondered if my story was good enough, smart enough, or interesting enough. Instead, I thought about what was going to happen next because, as I typed, the story was revealed to me.

I call this experience—it was about nine months—the Divine Download because I had no idea where this story was coming from. It emerged from somewhere inside of me in large chunks and pieces. I did my best to keep my fingers typing so I could capture it all.

My husband saw this happening and supported me. I did not try to fight it. I surrendered to it, and he helped. It was beyond "flow"; it was an experience of allowing my story to come forward. I lit a candle on my desk, listened to two songs from my Pandora playlist, repeated my Quality (Courage), and typed like a madwoman.

How did I fall into the Divine Download? I went through a major transformation in how I related to my writing and to myself as a writer. I cleared out tons of limiting beliefs and began treating myself and my writing with respect and honor. I experienced writing as a joy and not a measuring stick. I believe when the story found an opening, it poured forth onto the page in one of the most joyous, creative experiences I have ever had in my life.

After I wrote the novel and revised it many, many times, I hired a professional editor. She gave me critical feedback and I went back and revised the story again. And then I revised it some more. Finally, I sent out my manuscript to literary agents and secured representation. I was thrilled and thought, *I am on my way.* Then things got tricky.

The agent and I did not have good communication. After a year, I left the agent. At this point, I had a decision to make: how was I going to proceed? I had lunch with a former writing teacher and went over all the issues with her: the joy of writing the novel, the excitement of getting representation, the disappointment of it not working out, and the decision I had to make about what to do next.

My former teacher looked at me and said, "Whatever you decide to do, publishing your novel will change your life."

I decided to publish my first novel, *Restless in L.A.,* with a small publisher. I had a book launch party in Los Angeles at the venerable Book Soup in West Hollywood. A hundred friends and family showed up. The *Los Angeles Times* did a half-page story about my experience publishing a debut novel at age forty-seven.

After that, I met women at book clubs, literary events, and workshops who shared with me their writing dreams. I launched *Heart. Soul. Pen.* women's writing workshops to help other women find their voice shortly thereafter. I was filled with enthusiasm, confidence, and creativity. I did not just find my voice; I found my purpose. My path which had wound circuitously through public health, women's health, spiritual psychology, writing, parenting, and teaching suddenly made sense. I do not believe I would have found my purpose had I not started writing.

On the night of my book launch at Book Soup, I remember feeling extremely anxious. *What if I am not good enough? What if my reading is not smooth? What if people do not like the book or me or the evening?* It was the same questions I felt the day of my belly dance performance back when I was in spiritual psychology school. I reminded myself that I simply needed to show up as *myself.* That was enough. And it was. The event was a success. I sold books, everyone had a fantastic time, and the clerk at the bookstore told me she had never seen a launch event quite like mine; it was a joyous celebration.

Earlier in this book, I said that your project is always you— the writing is a byproduct. The night of my book launch I realized that more than ever. My project was to *show up fully as myself.* Writing and publishing the novel was the method by which I did it.

I cannot tell you what you will learn about yourself through your writing journey. I cannot predict if you will write a novel, memoir, one-woman show, book of poetry, or a treasured journal. But I can tell you that writing will bring you into a fuller relationship to yourself. You will find your voice on the page. And, once you find it, a shift happens, and you lean into your intuition and have greater confidence in your thoughts and feelings because you are more aware of what they are. Finding your voice changes not just your writing but your life.

If the Divine Download seems awesome to you—and it is!—I encourage you wholeheartedly to follow the nine steps that lead up to it. Before you start writing, prepare by revising your beliefs so they support you. Anchor to a Quality as you write and let it be your life raft. Create a writing ritual to invite in the magic and make space for yourself that is private. Enter into Curiosity and Discovery. Do not allow having an agenda spoil your writing freedom.

Remind yourself that writing is an adventure. Like a mountain climber, you are wedging your foot into one spot and searching for a handhold and then moving, body pressed against the mountain, to the next spot, looking for the next space for your feet, and the next hold for your hand. You are climbing your mountain. You are fierce, committed, and do not need to know how close or far the other climbers are from you or how fast they are moving. You just climb, feel the wind in your hair, the sun on your face, and keep moving. When you set a timer and write as fast as you can without thinking or judging, you are off. You are immersed in your adventure.

It does not matter where you are going, it just matters *that* you are going. When you have been sitting in the same spot for a long while or wandering around with no idea where you are, then being immersed in an adventure is a gift and you just write-write-write and let the words come out. Unleash your radical self-expression as fast as you can, and you will feel the wind in your hair.

Later, you follow the TIDES and look for triggers and keep digging, admiring, and being curious until you have gone as far as you can on your own. Then you can ask for help and commit to how you are going to move forward on a regular basis, all the while remembering this is your journey, no one else's. Your voice has value. Period. The end. No one needs to bestow value upon you. You have bestowed it upon yourself. That is enough.

If you keep writing, connecting, and committing, you may find yourself swept into the Divine Download, where words are pouring out of you, and it is all you can do to keep up. Write it all down and do your best to let it emerge because being in the flow is a precious experience. When it comes for you, I suggest going full force for the ride.

Here is a little secret: the Divine Download cannot happen if you do not write. If you have words inside of you that want to be unleashed, you have to sit down and proclaim to all parts of yourself, *I am available.* When you support yourself regularly with your pen, do not be surprised if the Divine Download appears. You do not have to know what form your Divine Download will take. Your work will tell you what it is. Don't look up. Don't look down. "Don't think. Just write."

CHAPTER TAKEAWAYS

- You are a writer because you were born a writer.
- You are a writer if you scribble quickly into a spiral notebook.
- You are a writer if you type into a laptop.

HEART. SOUL. PEN.

- You are a writer if no one sees you writing.
- You are a writer if everyone sees you writing.
- You are writer if you write in your bedroom, basement, or garage.
- You are a writer if you post your writing or if you don't.
- You are a writer if no one knows it but you.
- A writer is one who writes. Are you writing? Then you are a writer.

CHAPTER ELEVEN

A META MOMENT

I remember first grade when you told me I wasn't the star. When you took my gold ribbon off my little white shirt with the ruffles and gave it to someone else because I didn't deserve it. I remember when I was fourteen and I sang and bared everything in my young vulnerable heart to you but backstage you said I was too opinionated to ever get anything I wanted. I remember taking off my makeup and seeing my face for the first time. I remember shaving my long hair off with fear that I might see a monster but instead I saw beauty and a huge irrepressible smile.

—Jett F.
Prompt: *I remember*
Timer: 5 minutes

REPRISE

While I was writing this book, I was having an inherently "meta" moment. I was writing a book about writing a book while simultaneously experiencing what I was writing about.

When I first dove into writing *HEART. SOUL. PEN.*, I had fear and doubts. I wanted so much to write this book, but I was suddenly plagued with thoughts like: *What if I cannot do this? How will I crystallize this information? What if I cannot get it onto the page? What if I do not make my deadline? What if it is too hard?*

Step #1—Revise and Release Limiting Beliefs

As I was writing Step #1 about Revising Limiting Beliefs, I realized I was filled with limiting beliefs! I shook my head as I stopped and wrote out all the limiting beliefs that were holding me back and making me feel like I was not capable of writing this book. I was experiencing the feeling of writing through mud that I talk about in these pages. So I stopped and did the exercises in Step #1. I revised and released my limiting beliefs and created new beliefs that reinforced my ability, enthusiasm, and delight in writing *HEART. SOUL. PEN.*

My new beliefs looked like this:

- I am filled with wonder and curiosity as my book emerges from my heart onto the page.
- Now is the perfect time.
- I am enough.

- What I have to share has value.

- I am writing for my learning and upliftment.

- I am a channel of creativity.

- I am effortlessly allowing my words to emerge in service to liberating my voice and the voice of anyone who reads this book.

- My belief in the value of women's voices is a gift I offer to anyone who needs this message.

- I have a learning orientation to writing and to life.

The simple process of rewriting my beliefs made me feel lighter. I felt joy and anticipation stir inside me.

Step #2—Anchor to a Creative Quality

At Step #2: Anchor to a Quality, I thought about the book and the kind of support I needed. When I scanned the Deck of Qualities, I immediately knew I needed Flow. That was my anchor. I combined a few other Qualities to create: *Joyful Enthusiastic Flow.* That felt right. I did not want to force the words out of me or push them around a narrow cork of judgment. I wanted writing to be easy, joyful, and fun.

I wrote down my Quality and kept it next to my desk. Before I went to bed, I read *Joyful Enthusiastic Flow.* When I woke up, I read *Joyful Enthusiastic Flow.* When I sat down to write, I anchored to *Joyful Enthusiastic Flow.* When I was eating dinner and the book would come into my mind, I would sometimes hear doubt and fear. I saw them as little gremlins sitting at the table discussing my project and saying, "I don't think she can do it," and the other would say, "She should give up."

There I was, sitting at my kitchen table, eating a chicken breast and roasted Brussel sprouts and listening to doubt and fear in my head. When I realized what was happening, I conjured my Quality: *Joyful Enthusiastic Flow* and imagined I was spraying it through a hose at the doubt and fear gremlins. Not only did my Quality wash away the doubt and fear, but the whole imaginary drama made me laugh. My Quality as my anchor was present with me every minute of the day, as I sat at my laptop in my office, at the coffee shop, in my backyard, on my couch, or wherever I was writing-writing-writing, *Joyful Enthusiastic Flow* came with me.

Step #3—Create a Writing Ritual

For Step #3, I created a three-step writing ritual for myself:

1. I read my Quality of *Joyful Enthusiastic Flow* written on a neon orange note stuck to a Kleenex box on my desk.
2. I sat quietly for a one-minute meditation while envisioning my Quality pulsing through my body.
3. I played *Wonderwall* by Oasis two times.

This was the ritual I performed before I began writing. By the time I was finished with my second listening of *Wonderwall*, I felt so filled up with words I was bursting. I had not planned for the song or the meditation to be part of my ritual. It just felt right. There is no wrong way to design your ritual. This is what worked for me, so I went with it.

Step #4—Write Faster Than You Think

I was writing from an outline, so I wrote out all the lessons and stories that I knew were going to go into the book. Then I moved to Step #4 and wrote faster than I could think. I used a lesson I wanted to convey as a writing prompt. I set a timer for thirty minutes and let my words pour out. I unleashed all the thoughts and exercises I wanted to share while madly typing to a timer so that I did not get stuck and have to squeeze my words around a cork of judgment.

Step #5—Enter into Curiosity and Discovery

I noticed how I struggled with Step #5: Enter into Curiosity and Discovery. I was attached to the outcome. I wanted my writing to become the basis for this book. The more I focused on hitting all the key points, the harder writing became. I felt like I lost my flow. I was clinging to my Quality. As I was writing Step #5, I said to myself, *just be curious about what is coming out. Everything you want to say in this book is inside of you. Just surrender. Let it emerge.*

This shift helped me so much. Suddenly I was back in the flow and writing easily and, although I was loosely following the outline, I was letting the words emerge without being dictatorial. I was surprised by the thoughts and ideas that came forward. Sometime during Step #5, I noticed how much I was enjoying writing this book.

Step #6—Follow the TIDES

When I was done with each section of timed writing, I moved on to Step #6, looked at what I had written, and followed the TIDES. I paid particularly close attention to the themes, images, and details that were emerging. I might have thought I was going to write about summoning support, but what came out was a section about being curious. I was not getting attached to what I was writing. I was attached to the fact that I *was* writing. My job with my first draft was not to write a perfect book or a complete book—my job was to surrender to the perfection of allowing my creativity to come forward.

I knew I could edit and revise and structure the sections later. I looked at the trigger lines. What part of this story was I not telling? Where could I share more deeply about the writing process, about my process, about what I have come to know about women and writing? I went back and noticed what I noticed and looked for areas where I could dive deeper.

Step #7—Make and Keep Creative Commitments

Although I teach Step #7: Make and Keep Creative Commitments and review this concept every week during the writing courses I teach, I struggled with this on my own. I was on a tight deadline made tighter by wanting to get the first draft done early to give myself ample time for notes and editing. Even though I knew that making and keeping creative commitments was not a race, I was racing. I judged how much I got done each day and this caused tension inside of me.

I was literally writing sentences like, "This requires gentleness," and, "Be willing to change course and to do so in a way that is supportive and kind to yourself," and "Do not judge not achieving your goal as a failure. Instead see it as an opportunity for course correction." While at that very moment, I was not being gentle to myself and driving myself too hard. While I was writing about being willing to change course and do it in a way that is kind, I was yelling at myself to stick to my daily schedule.

As I was working on writing Step #7, I started to laugh, recognizing that I am not just the teacher of *HEART. SOUL. PEN.,* I am also a student of *HEART. SOUL. PEN.* I had to relearn core tenets of the program—it was time to be gentle, course correct, and do it with kindness. I needed to remind myself of this because I had forgotten.

Step #8—Share with Intention

I wrote and rewrote, and revised and revised again. I worked until I could not take the initial draft any further. Then it was time for Step #8: Share with Intention. For me, this was easy. I sent the newly completed manuscript to a fellow writer for strength-based feedback. I asked her to provide me with strength-based notes. I was particularly interested in where I could go deeper, where she had questions, and what she might want to know more about. I received notes that helped me go back into the manuscript with a new perspective. Her feedback energized me.

Step #9—Own Your Worthiness

I learned on control columns as I was going through the process of writing and publishing this book. I worked at keeping my attention and my efforts in the column of *What I Can Control* and not getting swept into *What I Cannot Control* when I was disappointed, discouraged, or frustrated. I knew I was not responsible for outcomes, but I had to constantly remind myself. The same was true when outside circumstances did go the way I hoped. I would feel grateful, thrilled, and delighted, but I wanted to remind myself not to attach my value to how the outside world received my work. External validation is fun, but it is not the truth.

Step #10—Receive the Divine Download

I knew the Divine Download hit me when I was still in my pajamas at 4 p.m. I did not have children to pick up at school anymore so 2:30 p.m. came and went and I was still in my office, dog at my feet, typing and hungry and wearing my robe. As I was madly swept into the flow, the mail was in the mailbox, the phone went unanswered, there was no food in the fridge, and no plans for dinner. Nothing could pull me out of my portal. Nothing could cut off the words that were pouring forth as I sat and wrote until my tailbone hurt and I had to buy a standing desk so I could stand and keep going. I was a vessel for words to pour forth from some magical place I did not know. When I looked up, the first draft of *HEART. SOUL. PEN.* was on the page!

A FINAL NOTE OF ENCOURAGEMENT

My message to you is to keep going. Create beliefs about your writing that support you, anchor to a Quality, and consider developing a short writing ritual to set you up for success. Quickly choose a prompt to start off your writing or select a drop-in prompt or both. Do not consider your prompts for long; just grab one and get started. Set your timer for five or ten or twenty minutes and write without stopping until the timer goes off. Commit to entering into Curiosity and Discovery while you write. Let go of having any agenda for your writing. Allow yourself to unleash your radical self-expression. After you write, follow the TIDES and identify trigger lines to go deeper. Get excited to write more often and see your writing as essential to your well-being. Create a regular writing practice. Consider sending your work out into the world. Always remember that YOU are the expert of your work and the arbiter of your value.

No one can tell your story but you. You are the only person who can unleash your radical self-expression. It matters. You matter. Make the time and space to find your voice on the page. It will not only change your writing; it will change your life.

KEEP IN TOUCH!

It is my hope that the end of this book is the beginning of your *HEART. SOUL. PEN.* journey. I invite you to continue your adventure by joining the *HEART. SOUL. PEN.* global community of women who come together to write, unleash their radical self-expression, and support one another. Join us at www.heart soulpen.com for events, classes, and workshops throughout the year. Keep in touch with me on Facebook and Instagram @robinfinnauthor or visit me at robinfinn.com and keep me posted on your writing progress. Creativity, community, and connection are the keys to fostering your writing momentum.

Loneliness is a serious public health issue. If you are longing to develop new and deeper relationships with others, I strongly recommend you consider starting your own *HEART. SOUL. PEN.* writing group. Gather together a group of creative women and write and share your words in community. At the end of this book, I have included a sample agenda, guidelines, and writing prompts to get you started. Follow the steps to a Divine Download of your own.

Most of all, keep writing, keep owning your worthiness, and keep supporting yourself as you find our voice on the page and in your life. Your words are worthy. Your story matters. You are worth it!

PART IV

HEART. SOUL. PEN. IN ACTION

WORKING THE PROCESS

E ach chapter of this book begins with a five-minute piece of timed writing from a different writer. Each writer was assigned the task of setting their timer for five minutes, beginning with the prompt "I remember," and writing as fast as they could the entire time without stopping until the timer went off. As with all heart writing, writers set the intention to be curious, to discover, and to release attachment to any outcome or agenda. Writers were not instructed *to remember* anything. In fact, their piece did not need to be about memory at all. I simply asked them to begin writing with "I remember," anchor to a sense of curiosity and discovery, and allow their words to emerge without editing, directing, crossing out, or judging.

You can see that each piece is unique. Every writer has a different voice. Each vignette veers into its own territory. Yet every piece contains the seeds of future stories. These chapter-opening pieces are five-minute writing assignments. So often writers are surprised by how much story can emerge in five short minutes. Heart writing drops you deeply into your material. With no agenda and no judgment, deep, fresh, raw material pours forth onto the page, even when you have five minutes. There are seeds planted in each piece that can be further explored if the writer so chooses. Any of this material could become a building block for a larger project.

Your freshly emerged writing is not *bad* or *nothing* or *junk*. It is fresh material. It simply needs to be acknowledged, not critiqued. If you choose to, your writing can be mined for deeper meaning by reviewing it through a strength-based lens, following the TIDES, and looking for trigger lines.

As we talked about at many different stages of our journey, shifting your lens to see the strengths in your writing is a practice. It takes time to become accustomed to this manner of inquiry. Instead of looking at what is wrong, or not good, or does not make sense, we can view our writing as an opportunity for discovery. Strength-based feedback is a powerful way to offer notes to fellow writers as well. You can follow the TIDES in other people's writing to provide feedback that encourages and inspires them. Below, we examine the chapter-opening excerpts in greater detail. Let's practice following the TIDES and identifying trigger lines together:

EXAMPLES: FOLLOW THE TIDES AND TRIGGERS

1) I remember my father. I wear his wedding ring on my pointer finger. I remember the sound of his voice and the jeans he used to wear and the white sneakers on his feet as he stepped into the canal to push the boat off the trailer and into the water so we could go fishing. I remember once how I came home late, like two in the morning, and I saw my father's car was not on the driveway. I knew he was driving around looking for me. I knew I was in big trouble. I was glad he did not find me behind Wags smoking weed with a police officer I met at a party he had come to break up. We got to talking, and the next thing I know, we were behind Wags smoking a joint. I do not know what would have made my dad angrier, the hour or the pot or the police officer. Actually, I do know: the police officer. I am glad I did not get caught behind Wags with Officer What's-his-name, I don't remember.

- **Theme**—What themes are coming forward? Youth, freedom
- **Images**—What images strike you? The wedding ring on the pointer finger, empty driveway
- **Details**—What details do you notice? White sneakers, the canal, Wags
- **Emotions**—What emotions are present in the writing? Loss, wistfulness
- **Structure**—What do you notice about the structure of the piece? Begins and end with not remembering
- Trigger lines: Are there lines that stand out as having more to say? Are there lines that could be used as prompts to uncover more story? I was in big trouble, I did not get caught

2) I remember when flying used to be a pleasure. The only thing we had to contend with was inclement weather. I

remember methodically planning trips with excitement and anticipation. Now, I do a balance transfer, borrow points, and redeem my vacation. I remember looking through my closet to choose a fabulous airplane outfit. These days, I don comfy jeggings, Uggs, and blanket to stave off being frostbit. I remember flying Eastern Airlines, checking bags, and eating a full meal, all for one inclusive fare. Today, I had to pay for my seat, carry-on, legroom, a box full of nuts. I remember chatting with my flight mates, collecting business cards, or happily looking out the window. Here, no connection, technology over humanity, plugged-in seatmate hitting me with his elbow. I remember wearing belts and shoes, paper tickets, meeting or greeting loved ones at the gate. This morning, at JFK, even with TSA pre-check, I was scanned twice and there were armed soldiers poised to keep us safe. Mostly, I remember traveling with ease, hope, tomato juice, and without panic disorder. The contrasts and new hassles are stark. Flying, nostalgically back in the past, I'd like to reorder.

- **Theme**—What themes are coming forward? Technology over humanity

- **Images**—What images strike you? Seatmate hitting her with his elbow, paper tickets, writer looking in her closet for her plane outfit

- **Details**—What details do you notice? Uggs, box full of nuts, belts, shoes, armed soldiers, tomato juice

- **E**motions—What emotions are present in the writing? Stress, anxiety, longing for the past
- **S**tructure—What do you notice about the structure of the piece? Piece traveled from pleasure to panic disorder
- Trigger lines: Are there lines that stand out as having more to say? Are there lines that could be used as prompts to uncover more story? I had to pay, I would like to reorder

3) I remember it was twilight on the day my husband died. The ICU nurse came in to move him from the chair back to his hospital bed. As he lifted him, my husband's legs gave out. I remember the nurse lowered him back to the chair and running out of the room. I remember my husband managed to raise his head and look at me. I remember how he was adamant that even though he was on the heart transplant list, he would not be leaving the medical center alive. I remember how his eyes locked into mine—knowing his heart was finally done with a long and difficult fight. In nanoseconds, I saw surprise and fear and a beseeching incredulity that felt like he needed me to take care of this. The connection was broken when a horde of doctors and nurses stampeded into his room. I remember someone rushed me out. I remember I let them. I remember how cold the seat of the folding chair was as I sat waiting for the children to arrive. I

remember a doctor suddenly appearing, masked, and wearing gloves. I remember praying for the kids to get there.

- **T**heme—What themes are coming forward? Loss, control

- **I**mages—What images strike you? ICU nurse lifting patient, eyes locking, cold seat of the folding chair

- **D**etails—What details do you notice? Twilight, heart transplant list, horde of doctors and nurses, mask, gloves

- **E**motions—What emotions are present in the writing? Grief, loneliness, sorrow

- **S**tructure—What do you notice about the structure of the piece? The piece had a beginning, middle, and end

- Trigger lines: Are there lines that stand out as having more to say? Are there lines that could be used as prompts to uncover more story? I sat waiting, he needed me to take care of this

4) I remember what it used to be like before everyone died. It's sad to think about, I know. But life has been a storm of loss lately, so death and mortality are on my mind 24/7. It's sad to have lost so much in such a short time. First our two cats. Then Grandma. Then our foster kitten. Then my mother-in-law. I am trying not to wait for the other shoe to drop, but it seems

the floodgates have opened, and everyone around us continues to pass. But that's just life, isn't it? We're born. We live. We die. It's sad, but I guess it doesn't have to be. Before everyone died, we felt untouchable. Like death was just something far, far away. I wasn't afraid of it. I knew it would come someday, but that day was at least seventy years away. And now that we've lost so many, it feels like death is around every corner. Maybe it is. But that's just death, isn't it? It's sad and it's hard to reckon with, but I guess it doesn't have to be. Grandma's passing was slow and agonizing. My mother-in-law's passing was quick and agonizing. Yet both of them went with grace and peace. Neither went with fear or dread or regrets. And both of them passed with the people who loved them most by their sides. Death is sad, but when you've lived a full life and have people to show for it, I guess it doesn't have to be. So I'll try not to be afraid of dying.

- **Theme**—What themes are coming forward? Mortality, the human condition
- **Images**—What images strike you? The floodgates open, two cats
- **Details**—What details do you notice? Grandma, foster kitten, mother-in-law, seventy years away, a short time
- **Emotions**—What emotions are present in the writing? Fear of death, grief, sadness,

- **S**tructure—What do you notice about the structure of the piece? The movement from feeling untouchable to feeling afraid of dying

- Trigger lines: Are there lines that stand out as having more to say? Are there lines that could be used as prompts to uncover more story? I am trying not to wait for the other shoe to drop, I'll try not to be afraid of dying.

5) I remember when I found out I was pregnant with my daughter. My husband and I had been intimate one time because life was already hectic with a three-year-old. I recall looking at the calendar and thinking, did I get my period? I couldn't remember because I was laid off from my job and currently looking for a teaching position. But I went down to the store and got a pregnancy test, and my thoughts went wild: There is no way I am pregnant! We can't be pregnant, right? We only did it ONE time. Am I extra fertile? Then I took the test and thought I really have to be overreacting right now. Then I saw the two lines and said, "Holy shit! I don't believe it." Then I got the call for the job interview. The woman on the phone said, "We want to interview you." I made it clear, "Oh you don't want to hire me. I just found out I'm pregnant." She went on to say, "Well, we can't legally discriminate against you." I hear you but starting out as a first-year teacher in middle school while pregnant is something that I didn't want to do. She went on, "We have resources for you to go on maternity

leave. Just come in and see if you are the right fit." So I
did. But in my mind, I thought I really don't want this
to happen and how am I going to raise two children and
be a first-year teacher?

- **Theme**—What themes are coming forward? Over-
  whelm, life's surprises
- **Images**—What images strike you? Looking at
  the calendar, the two lines of the pregnancy test,
  shocked narrator discovering she is pregnant
- **Details**—What details do you notice? Three-year-
  old, one time, the store, the pregnancy test, maternity leave
- **Emotions**—What emotions are present in the writing? Shock, surprise, trepidation
- **Structure**—What do you notice about the structure
  of the piece? The piece had a beginning, middle,
  and end
- Trigger lines: Are there lines that stand out as having more to say? Are there lines that could be used as
  prompts to uncover more story? I don't believe it, I
  really don't want this to happen.

EXERCISE: YOUR TURN

Review the following six pieces, follow the TIDES, and identify trigger lines you see in each piece. At the end of each, ask
yourself what you notice and answer the questions below.

1) I remember when my new therapist told me I was
depressed. I said, "No, I'm not." She laughed. And
laughed. And laughed. I have been in therapy since
I was eighteen years old. I have never had a therapist
quite like this one and I have had several therapists over
the years. My longest relationship was with a therapist
I worked with at my office through the EAP program.
She helped me when I got promoted. Then she helped
me with my life when I got divorced. She helped me
envision what I wanted and once even hypnotized me.
I remember the vision—I was standing in a field of tall
grasses and there was a yellow sunny haze over the scene.
I was wearing a long flowing skirt and I was with a man
who was lifting up a little baby with light blonde hair
toward the sky. That vision came true. I got married
and had a baby. And I was happy. But between the pandemic, menopause, losing a job, selling a house, a close
friend passing, financial pressures, and applying to high
school for that baby, I became depressed. I didn't realize
it though. I stopped painting. I stopped going to yoga.
I stopped meditating. When my new therapist stopped
laughing, she said, "You are depressed, and I am going
to help you come out of it. You are going to buy new

art supplies and go to yoga and start meditating again."
And you know what? I did all those things and now,
nine months later, I can look back and say, that yes, I
was depressed, and I can only laugh.

- **T**heme—What themes are coming forward?
- **I**mages—What images strike you?
- **D**etails—What details do you notice?
- **E**motions—What emotions are present in the writing?
- **S**tructure—What do you notice about the structure of the piece?
- Trigger lines: Are there lines that stand out as having more to say? Are there lines that could be used as prompts to uncover more story?

2) I remember when I used to run. Well maybe it was
more of a jog. I eventually did three miles several times
a week. I was in great shape, younger then too. I would
wear two sports bras so my double Ds wouldn't bounce
all over the place. It helped. I would suit up, depending on the weather. Leggings, T-shirt, sometimes a long
sleeve T with hooks for my thumbs so the sleeves covered my hands the slightest bit too. That's for when it
was cooler out. I'd put on a baseball hat, my orange
one with *Alaska* written on the front, a souvenir from
a family cruise years earlier. I'd put in my headphones
and music from my little pink iPod nano (I think it was

called) would play, motivating me with various beats (Madonna's "Ray of Light," Rage Against the Machine's "Renegades of Funk," Justin Timberlake—anything!, maybe even some One Direction) and I would jog through the neighborhood in a familiar loop. My sister encouraged me, "Just start out a little bit at a time, stop when you need to, push yourself a little more every time you go . . ." and it worked. One of the few times she ever even gave me advice that I either asked for or just listened to when she offered it.

- **T**heme—What themes are coming forward?
- **I**mages—What images strike you?
- **D**etails—What details do you notice?
- **E**motions—What emotions are present in the writing?
- **S**tructure—What do you notice about the structure of the piece?
- Trigger lines: Are there lines that stand out as having more to say? Are there lines that could be used as prompts to uncover more story?

3) I remember the feel of the hot tea and its sweetness as it ran down my throat and straight into my bloodstream, the taste of the tuna sandwich, its substance the equivalent in that moment of a full roast beef dinner with all the trimmings, including a Yorkshire pudding covered in gravy. The nurses had covered me in a warm

blanket, the blood covering the floor just to the side of the bed had come from my body only thirty minutes earlier. I didn't look now, but I remembered watching the midwife tug on the umbilical cord after the baby had finally been born. She was frantic because my body, exhausted, would not expel the placenta. Then the blood came, and the doctor pushed me back onto the bed and inserted a drug to induce my body, unwilling, to release the baby's empty home from my uterus before it could kill me. A tiredness was settling into me that would last for months. It hadn't been until I was given a catheter to drain my bladder that the hours of pushing led to the immediate swoosh of the baby down the birth canal and out of my body and into his father's hands. I knew I should be happy, relieved, elated but I was overwhelmed. I focused on the sweet tea and sandwich, the very best meal I have ever eaten in my life.

- **Theme**—What themes are coming forward?
- **Images**—What images strike you?
- **Details**—What details do you notice?
- **Emotions**—What emotions are present in the writing?
- **Structure**—What do you notice about the structure of the piece?
- Trigger lines: Are there lines that stand out as having more to say? Are there lines that could be used as prompts to uncover more story?

4) I remember the feel of my grandmother's soft velvety cheek. The way it felt against mine as she held my head between her hands and pulled me in to kiss my cheek and then rest hers against mine. The smell of her Jean Nate body soap that enveloped me in her embrace. She had sparkling blue eyes and wore her salt and pepper hair in two long braids that she crossed over the top of her head and were held in place with tortoise shell hair pins. She was not a big woman, maybe 5'4" at the most, and yet, she gave birth to 6 giants, all boys and all over 6 feet tall. My own father topped them all at 6'7". She was born in Eindhoven in the Netherlands in 1901. As a young woman, she met my grandfather while working as a chemist for Phillips. He was a widow nearly twenty years her senior, having lost his wife in childbirth, and now was a single father raising his daughter alone. They lived and raised their boys in Eindhoven until 1936 when my grandfather, fearing the rise of Hitler, decided to leave everything behind and move his family to the United States.

- **T**heme—What themes are coming forward?
- **I**mages—What images strike you?
- **D**etails—What details do you notice?
- **E**motions—What emotions are present in the writing?
- **S**tructure– What do you notice about the structure of the piece?

- Trigger lines: Are there lines that stand out as having more to say? Are there lines that could be used as prompts to uncover more story?

5) I remember that the pressure in my sinuses makes me want to lie down and there is something in my jack-o-lantern stretch pants that is poking into my inner thigh and these two sensations are causing me severe distress. There are these goddamn mosquitoes, and they swirl around my head as I do my Peloton workout and make me anxious in my downward dog and I reach and clap and try to squish them between my hands and make a loud clapping sound which startles the dog. I remember to eat lunch with my dad and my brother and my stepdad. I told my husband that if he and my son had been at the restaurant then every single important man in my life would have been present. We ate chips and salsa, although I did not eat chips and salsa because I make it a rule not to eat chips and salsa or French fries or donuts or cheap birthday cake at kids' parties. These rules used to work, and I was able to maintain a reasonable weight and fit into my mom jeans, but something has happened in the past year or so and the flesh has gathered around my middle. While my face still looks normal in pictures, the jeans do not fit and that's why I wear festive leggings and try to divert people's attention away from my midsection by tying a jean jacket or sweatshirt around my waist. But this strategy does not work and only makes me look slovenly.

- **T**heme—What themes are coming forward?
- **I**mages—What images strike you?
- **D**etails—What details do you notice?
- **E**motions—What emotions are present in the writing?
- **S**tructure—What do you notice about the structure of the piece?
- Trigger lines: Are there lines that stand out as having more to say? Are there lines that could be used as prompts to uncover more story?

6) I remember first grade when you told me I wasn't the star. When you took my gold ribbon off my little white shirt with the ruffles and gave it to someone else because I didn't deserve it. I remember when I was fourteen and I sang and bared everything in my young vulnerable heart to you, but backstage you said I was too opinionated to ever get anything I wanted. I remember taking off my makeup and seeing my face for the first time. I remember shaving my long hair off with fear that I might see a monster, but instead I saw beauty and a huge irrepressible smile.

- **T**heme—What themes are coming forward?
- **I**mages—What images strike you?
- **D**etails—What details do you notice?
- **E**motions—What emotions are present in the writing?

- **S**tructure—What do you notice about the structure of the piece?

- Trigger lines: Are there lines that stand out as having more to say? Are there lines that could be used as prompts to uncover more story?

STARTING A SUCCESSFUL *HEART. SOUL. PEN.* WRITING GROUP

THE THREE CS: COMMUNITY, CREATIVITY, AND CONNECTION

Writing is a solitary gig. You sit at your desk and type away alone, except for your dog or cat or bird, if you have one. If you are like me, when you are in "the flow," you might not even get out of your pajamas. Even if you get dressed and leave the house to write in a library or coffee shop, you still write in your own personal vacuum. Because writing requires that you spend significant time alone, common obstacles that can derail a thriving writer's life can be loneliness, lack of inspiration, and the inability to prioritize your writing. Creating a *HEART. SOUL. PEN.* writing group can help counter these obstacles and supercharge your writing practice by addressing the three Cs: community, creativity, and connection.

Community

Women often have friend groups: our work friends, our kid friends, our couple friends. Adding a new category of "writer friends" to our lives means incorporating a community of people with whom we can talk about writing and share our creative struggles and successes. Writer friends know you in a different way than other friends. They see and hear and recognize you through your work. It is an intimate relationship of a different type that both enriches your writing and expands the roles you play in your life: mother, daughter, sister, friend, writer. Even though you continue to write, edit, and revise alone at your kitchen table or at a local coffee shop, you have a community of friends cheering you on and rooting for your success. The impact of community cannot be overstated.

In his bestselling book *Outliers: The Story of Success*,[1] the journalist and writer Malcom Gladwell shared the story of a group of people from the town of Roseto, Pennsylvania, who lived extraordinarily healthier and longer lives than their neighbors because of one simple and stunning reason: *community.* The people of Roseto were deeply intertwined in each other's lives. They came from the same small town in Italy and lived with a sense of trust, security, and support. This led not just to better health outcomes but to increased longevity. If feeling supported and connected can increase your lifespan, you can imagine the effect it can have on your creative self-expression. Creating or joining a *HEART. SOUL. PEN.* writing group adds a layer of trust, security, and support to your writing life. Following the steps and guidelines from the book will ensure the group is cooperative, not competitive, and that writers feel supported.

CREATIVITY

A common obstacle writers face is lack of inspiration. When we write alone, we often don't see the seeds for future stories we are sowing in our work, we get discouraged or bored or frustrated, and we give up. In a *HEART. SOUL. PEN.* writing group, we write together at each meeting and provide strength-based feedback to each writer. Everyone enjoys the benefits of writing in community and hearing from others what they notice in their writing, where it is strong, what strikes them, and where they can consider going deeper. When we write and share together on a regular basis, we consistently hear how our writing resonates for others. More often than not, this surprises and delights us and makes us eager to write more. Working with a strength-based lens also discourages competition and encourages support.

Judgment is a cork that stops our creative flow. Writing in a space defined by *HEART. SOUL. PEN.,* focused on safety, curiosity, discovery, and strength-based feedback, allows our creativity to fly free.

CONNECTION

Part of the magic of being in a writing group is that it keeps you connected to your writing goals and dreams. In a busy life, it can be hard to keep your eyes on the prize. Your burning desire to finish that story or write that essay or get back to work on your novel gets sidetracked by a child's illness, a work emergency, or a family vacation. You realize, months or even years later, that your writing project has languished. A nurturing writing group reminds you. They do not let you off the hook in the best of ways. It is harder to hide from yourself and your writing goals once you have shared them with a group and committed to them out loud. Your writer friends root for you and remind you that you are a writer and that you must make space in your life for writing, even when it is difficult to find the time.

Getting Started

Here are some tips to get your *HEART. SOUL. PEN.* writing group started:

- Find four to eight people with whom to launch your *HSP* group. With more than eight people, it can become difficult to allow time for each person to read and share. Often writers ask where the best place is to find members for a writing group. Classes and writing workshops you have attended are a good place to look. Also check out literary events at libraries and bookstores.

- Identify one person to moderate the group. It can be the same person or rotate each meeting but identifying who will guide the group keeps it moving along and ensures timing and guidelines are followed.

- Follow a planned agenda. You want to avoid spending time figuring out how to structure the meeting every time the group convenes. People naturally want to feel their time is well spent. You will get the most out of your writing group with consistent participation, so adhering to an established agenda brings value to the time spent together and encourages committed attendance.

Sample materials are available at the end of this chapter to kick off your writing group.

COMMON QUESTIONS ABOUT WRITING GROUPS

Below are common question writers ask about creating or joining writing groups:

- Do all the writers have to have the same writing interests? Not at all. Writing with others with vastly different interests and sensibilities is exciting and contributes to growth in both content and skills.
- How do you balance the different needs in a writing group where some people are fully committed, and others seem to barely engage? I suggest having a group of four to eight people so that if some participants are absent, you can still have a vibrant group. Over time, there is natural attrition. I recommend setting

expectations at the first meeting so participants can determine if the group is a good fit for them.

- Does a writing group need to be homogeneous in terms of novel genre or style? *Heart. Soul. Pen.* has always welcomed all genres and styles. I find that groups thrive with different genres, whether participants are writing fiction, personal essay, poetry, or stream-of-consciousness word flow, it's all good and we learn something unique from each person's self-expression. In fact, I think it contributes to the excitement of writing together.

SAMPLE AGENDA, GUIDELINES, WRITING PROMPTS

SAMPLE AGENDA

a Introductions (for the first class or when adding new members: share writing intentions and what you hope to get from the group)

b Choose a Quality and do a one-minute meditation

c Pick a writing prompt

d Timed heart writing exercise

e Each writer shares her work and receives strength-based feedback from the group

f Homework, if any

g Creative commitments: Did you make one? Did you keep it? Any need for course correction?

h Self-acknowledgment for showing up

Writing Group Guidelines

a No self-deprecating. Ever. No criticizing your writing, your work, or your creative process. Be neutral or positive only.

b When sharing, provide strength-based feedback only. No critique.

c All work is treated as fiction. Refer to the main character as "the narrator" or "the protagonist," not as "you."

d During feedback, the writer listens and does not answer questions. The writer may want to capture the notes she is receiving from the group for further development of her writing in the future.

e When sharing your work, emotions may come up. This is okay. Simply pause and wait until you are ready and finish reading your work.

f All participants should take the "Vegas Pledge" and, by show of hands, agree that what is written in writing group stays in writing group. This creates a safe container for your creativity.

Playful Writing Prompts for Groups

• Text messages: Look at your phone and choose the last line of your last text message. Share it with group. Do a ten-minute writing exercise beginning with the text message.

- Think of a state of being (examples include mothering/ moving/waking): Pick three words to describe this state. Share your words with the group. Do a ten-minute writing exercise and drop the three words somewhere into the writing.

- What's happening here: Choose an image from the Internet. What does this image say about your own life? Share the first thought that comes to mind with the group. Do a ten-minute writing exercise beginning with the thought the image inspired.

- Every object tells a story: Name three objects from any room in your home that speak to you about your life. Share the objects with the group. Do a ten-minute writing exercise and drop the three objects somewhere into the writing.

ACKNOWLEDGMENTS

This book would not have been written without the women who have showed up and shared their stories with me. A most heartfelt thanks to all the students, clients, workshop participants, and fellow writers who have made *HEART. SOUL. PEN.* possible. Your courage, creativity, and commitment has astounded and inspired me. My deepest love and gratitude to every single writer who has been a part of this journey.

To my literary agent, Michele Martin, you are a gem, and your tenacity and support is so greatly appreciated, and to Phil Marino for believing in this book.

To the Ladies Who Lit: thank you to Courtney Crane for your humor and Megan Austin Oberle for your always available ear and inspiring presence. Thank you to my friend and fellow author Melissa Gould, my MGA, for your unending love, support, and phone calls. Ladies, sharing our writing journeys and our friendship has enhanced my life.

I want to thank my spiritual teachers who have guided me along the path of self-discovery: Drs. Ron and Mary Hulnick and the University of Santa Monica, from whom I learned how to transform my inner and outer experience; my beloved mentor, Bella Mahaya Carter, who watered a seed just starting to grow and has shared her light and love ever since, and to Esther Hicks and Abraham, I could not have finished this manuscript without you.

To my students who so graciously contributed their thoughts and words to this book: Christina Airola, Cara Chalmers, Megan Dolan, Ilana Drucker, Rebecca Dupont, Laila Ferreira, Miranda Hyman, Dana Lee, and Dari Mackenzie, thank you for sharing your talent and the power of writing from the heart. To my longtime friend and beta reader Lisa Angerame, I am so grateful for your friendship, strength-based feedback, and support along this journey.

I could not have done it without my girlfriends who cheered me on as this book came into being: Carrie Augenstein, Carrie Kneitel, Natalie Shapiro, and Pam Tannenbaum; and to my dearest cheerleader extraordinaire Lorelle Taras, who was there from the beginning. It takes a village to manifest a dream. Thank you all for the love. And to Lila Gruzen for everything.

To my brothers, Michael Finn and Darren Finn, for your unwavering support and enthusiasm for everything I do.

To my beloved mother, Vicki Finn, one of the world's most avid readers. I will always miss you. Thank you for passing on your love of words. You would have loved this book! To my father, Ronnie Finn, I wish you were here to share the joy.

To my children: Miranda, my songbird and fellow creative searcher; Eli, my bright light that shines undaunted; Nick, my spirited artist and poet, you are my teachers and the great loves of my life. Thank you for always supporting me even when you had to await responses to your calls and text messages because

Acknowledgments

MOM IS WRITING, and for being so joyfully and wildly yourselves. You inspire me every day.

And to Michael, my favorite person on the planet, your support bolstered my courage, made my writing journey possible, and bathed my life in love. I could not possibly thank you for everything, but I will try. I love you.

NOTES

INTRODUCTION: WELCOME TO *HEART. SOUL. PEN.*

1. Claire Wasserman, *Ladies Get Paid: The Ultimate Guide to Breaking Barriers, Owning Your Worth, and Taking Command of Your Career* (New York: Gallery Books, 2021), 3.

CHAPTER ONE. STEP #1–REVISE AND RELEASE LIMITING BELIEFS

1. Ronald Hulnick, Mary Hulnick, and Neale Donald Walsch, *Loyalty to Your Soul: The Heart of Spiritual Psychology* (Carlsbad, CA: Hay House, February 2011).

CHAPTER THREE. STEP #3–CREATE A WRITING RITUAL

1. Francesca Gino and Michael I. Norton, "Why Rituals Work," *Scientific American,* May 14, 2013, https://www.scientificamerican.com/article/why-rituals-work.
2. Kent Sanders, "The Writing Routines of Five Famous Authors," Daily Writer, March 7, 2021, https://dailywriterlife.com/the-writing-routines-of-5-famous-authors/.
3. Noah Charney, "Elizabeth Gilbert: How I Write," Daily Beast, updated July 11, 2017, https://www.thedailybeast.com/elizabeth-gilbert-how-i-write.
4. Hope Reese, "Margaret Atwood Doesn't Read Reviews," The Cut, March 7, 2022, https://www.thecut.com/2022/03/how-margaret-atwood-gets-it-done.html.

5. Scarlett Harris, "Gillian Flynn Spends Her Days with Some Pretty Dark Characters," The Cut, July 10, 2023, https://www.thecut.com /2023/07/how-gillian-flynn-gets-it-done.html.

CHAPTER SIX. STEP #6–FOLLOW THE TIDES

1. Pat Schneider and Peter Elbow, *Writing Alone and with Others* (Oxford: Oxford University Press, 2003), xxii.

STARTING A SUCCESSFUL *HEART. SOUL. PEN.* WRITING GROUP

1. Malcolm Gladwell, *Outliers: The Story of Success* (Boston: Back Bay Books, 2011).

FURTHER READING

Ladies Get Paid: The Ultimate Guide to Breaking Barriers, Owning Your Worth, and Taking Command of Your Career by Claire Wasserman (New York: Gallery Books, 2021)

Loyalty to Your Soul: The Heart of Spiritual Psychology by Ronald Hulnick, Mary Hulnick, and Neale Donald Walsch (New York: Hay House, 2011)

Outliers: The Story of Success by Malcolm Gladwell (Boston: Back Bay Books, 2011)

Writing Alone and with Others by Pat Schneider and Peter Elbow (Oxford: Oxford University Press, 2003)

ABOUT THE AUTHOR

Photo by
Maria V. Cano-Mooradian

Robin Finn, MPH, MA, is passionate about sharing women's words. She is an award-winning writer, teacher, and coach, and the founder of Heart. Soul. Pen.® women's writing workshops and Hot Writing,™ where midlife and menopause inspire the desire to say what you mean without apologizing. Her work has appeared in national and international press, including the *New York Times, Washington Post, Los Angeles Times, BuzzFeed, Huffington Post*, and more. She teaches at UCLA Extension Writers' Program and offers workshops for women and organizations of all types. Robin is a cum laude graduate of UCLA and holds master's degrees in public health from Columbia University and in spiritual psychology from the University of Santa Monica. She lives in Los Angeles with her family and is a longtime advocate for children with ADHD and learning differences. Find her at www.robinfinn.com.

Printed in the USA
CPSIA information can be obtained
at www.ICGtesting.com
JSHW080451120524
62939JS00001B/1